Expandability of Investment Real Estate

Nikita S. Zhitov

Raleigh, North Carolina

ISBN:
ebook: 979-8-9927740-0-9
Paperback: 979-8-9927740-1-6
Hardcover: 979-8-9927740-2-3

Because of the dynamic nature of the Internet, any web addresses or links contained in this book may have changed since publication and may no longer be valid. The views expressed in this work are solely those of the author and do not necessarily reflect the views of the publisher, and the publisher hereby disclaims any responsibility for them.

Cover image licensed from Shutterstock.

Certain stock imagery licensed from Getty Images; people depicted in Getty Images stock imagery are models and are used for illustrative purposes only. Additional interior images created using artificial intelligence (AI) and personal images provided by the author.

Second Edition
Revision date: May 2025

CONTENTS

DISCLOSURE

This book is designed to provide information that the author believes to be accurate on the subject matter it covers, but it is sold with the understanding that the author is not offering individualized advice tailored to any specific portfolio or to any individual's particular needs or rendering investment advice or other professional services such as legal or accounting advice. A competent professional's services should be sought if one needs expert assistance in areas that include investment, legal, and accounting advice.

This publication references some historical transactions in which the author was involved. Past results do not guarantee future performance. Additionally, performance results, in addition to laws and regulations, change over time, which could change the accuracy of the information in this book. This book solely provides historical transactions of the author to discuss and illustrate the underlying principles. Additionally, this book is not intended to serve as the basis for any financial decision, as a recommendation of a specific investment advisor, or as an offer to sell or purchase any security. Only a prospectus and/or a private placement memorandum and/or a limited partnership agreement may be used to offer to sell or purchase securities, and the legal documents must be read and considered carefully before investing or spending money.

No warranty is made with respect to the accuracy or completeness of the information contained herein, and the author specifically disclaims any responsibility for any liability, loss, or risk, personal or otherwise, that is incurred as a consequence, directly or indirectly, of the use and application of any of the contents of this book.

INTRODUCTION

It is a known fact that real estate has created more millionaires than all other types of businesses combined. Unlike many businesses that are *not* backed by real assets, real estate investing in general is a sure way to build wealth over time. However, it is a very slow and lengthy process. Real estate typically requires a large upfront investment and a long waiting period before significant changes in your financial well-being become noticeable. Nevertheless, real estate has an unlimited potential to expedite such natural processes of long-term wealth creation so that significant changes in your wealth can become noticeable much sooner than might otherwise occur.

The value of income-producing properties is a function of the net operating income (NOI) and the market capitalization rate (CAP rate). If you search the web, you will find thousands of different definitions of what CAP rate is, none of which seem to be exactly the same and none of which seem to be correct, in my opinion. I think the simplest explanation of CAP rate is this—a market opinion of the perceived risk associated with an investment. The higher the risk, the higher the CAP rate. The lower the perceived risk, the lower the CAP rate.

Given that CAP rate is a collective market opinion of the perceived risk of an investment, there is little we can do as property owners to change such collective opinion. You could perhaps replace the tenants in your building with higher-credit tenants who are perceived to be less of a default risk, but that change is usually outside of your control and not easy to do in general.

So the real opportunity to create value and forced appreciation is through changes in the NOI rather than the CAP rate. NOI being a function of the income and expenses of the building gives us the opportunity to increase the property's value by either increasing the income or reducing the expenses of the property, both having a compound effect on NOI and value. This book will demonstrate examples of how small changes in the income or expense line items of your property can result in significant equity gain and cash flow.

When it comes to investment real estate, small changes in the income and expenses of a property yield large increases in value and equity. For example, a $100 per month increase in rental income on an income-producing property will result in a $20,000 instant equity increase in a 6.00% CAP market. However, it is also important to note that when you increase your income by $100, or say 10%, but your operating expenses of 35% do not change, the compound effect on NOI is not just 10% but rather 15.38%! So while you increased your rents only by 10%, your value has really increased by over 15.38%!

This book is designed for owners of real property to help identify potential cash flow-add and value-add opportunities and to provide inexpensive implementation tools to accelerate the process of wealth creation through long-term property ownership. New investors as well as sophisticated real estate entrepreneurs will benefit from implementing various small changes described in this book with minimum out-of-pocket cost and thus magnify the values and property cash flows for potentially multi-million dollar profits.

We live in a world of instant gratification, and people are generally impatient—me included. We do not want to wait; we want it now. An average payback period on an investment for a typical income-producing property in most markets across the United States takes 12-20 years. The instant gratification nature of our society makes real estate an unattractive investment strategy, especially for young investors or investors who otherwise are at the beginning of their path of wealth creation. For that reason, I hope that many real estate entrepreneurs will find this book useful, as the investment strategies described herein can help real estate investors of any level to potentially effect a significant and positive change to their cash flow, equity position, and overall financial well-being over a short period of time. These methods can propel a real estate investor to a new level of wealth—like they have done for me—that was otherwise perceived to be unachievable.

I began my real estate investment career at the age of 18, while living in the dormitory of my high school with less than $100 in my pocket. I had no family money, no endorsements, and no connections within the real estate industry or the business world in general. I was an immigrant student with minimal knowledge of the English language, and my circle of influence was limited to a bunch of carefree high schoolers and maybe a couple of professors.

So my career in real estate acquisition began at the lowest possible starting point. They say that necessity is the mother of invention. I guess this statement held true in my life. I wanted to not only survive; I wanted to get ahead in life. I knew that I had to become very creative if I was going to make it in real estate with no money, no credit, and no friends.

Yet, a clear understanding of how small changes in income or expenses in income-producing properties can have a compound effect on NOI allowed me to expedite the natural processes of long-term property ownership by hundreds and thousands of times. The understanding of this concept allowed me to not only survive in a world of volatile economies but also to do and to have almost everything I ever wanted in life. As of the date of this publication, I have acquired and/or developed several hundred properties worth many hundreds of millions of dollars. For that reason, I am a great believer in the creation of leverageable equities to accumulate as many real properties as possible, ideally using little of your own money.

My colleagues often refer to me as a master of creative deal structuring with no money out-of-pocket. After being full-time in the arena of real estate acquisitions for over 20 years, I have become a student of this sport. I have probably tried almost every possible way to create equity and cash flow out of pure "thin air." Every investment strategy described in this book is designed to be achieved with very little money out of your pocket. These strategies can be utilized by both new investors with very little cash and sophisticated investors with multi-billion-dollar portfolios. I hope you can pick up one or more ideas from this book that will help you improve your financial well-being and make you millions of dollars like these strategies have done for me.

I wish you the greatest of success in your real estate endeavors!

—Nikita Zhitov

ACKNOWLEDGEMENTS

Real estate is a team sport, and I strongly believe that an individual's success in this sport can be attributed to the people that surround the individual, not to the individual himself or herself. I would like to attribute my personal success, however small or large it may be, to those people who influenced me over the years and who helped me become who I am today.

First, I would like to thank my family—my parents, Sergey and Olga, and my older sister, Elena—for their inspiration and guidance these many years. Much of the philosophical content of this book originated from the principles that my parents instilled in me at a very young age. My sister helped me get through many difficult times of adversity during my late teens and early 20s, and you would most certainly not hold this book in your hands were it not for her. The most important ingredient of success in business is one that has nothing to do directly with business itself—peace and unconditional support at home; and without the one from my family, mine would have been nonexistent. Thank you, and I love you all very much!

I would also like to express my gratitude to my business partners at CityPlat, Vincenzo Verdino, Patrick Moore, and Gaurav Patel, for their unmatched work ethic and incredible tenacity in growing CityPlat from a 3-person startup company to a 9-figure AUM company it is today. Thank you for being good partners and for always contributing to the joint enterprise more than your fair share.

Also, I would like to thank my original mentors and teachers in the sport of real estate acquisition, Ron Pate and Greg Pinneo, who graciously took valuable time out of their busy schedules to provide guidance to a young immigrant real estate entrepreneur with no college education, no knowledge of real estate, finance, negotiations, life, or even a basic business sense—the person who I was at one time. Their knowledge of real estate, their wisdom of life principles and business ethics, their contribution to my character formation, and their support during the time of my many failures have helped shape my mindset to be able to see real estate through a different set of lenses. Your contribution to my knowledge base, my skills, and my abilities has been invaluable.

A special thanks goes to my many investment partners, friends, and advisors who supported me during hard times and good times, believed in me, invested with me, and provided their invaluable guidance as I navigated my course through the turbulent waters of commercial real estate. These people include, but are not limited to, Rafik Moore, Scott Scheel, Alex Lovi, Alan Schnur, Arnold Kozys, Saul Zenkevicius, Danny Newberry, Kevin Almolsch, Yuriy Vaynshteyn, Jon Anderson, Todd Saieed, Eli Zablud, Hisham Sabha, and Yazan Issa.

Finally, I'd like to thank my beautiful wife, Kristina, and my children, Lilya and Tima, for always supporting me and believing in me. Thank you for being patient and understanding as I sometimes take valuable time away from you to attend to my investment and business endeavors. I love you very much, and I hope you know that any minute of time spent outside of being with you is spent with the sole purpose of bettering your life, creating an abundance of opportunities for you, and creating freedom in your future.

1

Property Taxes

"Small changes in cash
flow create a huge difference
in equity."

PROPERTY TAXES : ENDLESS RESOURCE OF EQUITY CREATION

Most real property owners and/or investors do not think about property taxes as a potential source of savings or as a way to optimize net operating income (NOI). Property taxes are a necessary component associated with real property ownership, but they rarely elicit a positive consideration. When people receive a property tax bill, they assume that whatever is stated on the tax bill is what is owed and what they must pay. While this statement is true, the property tax bill—or rather a property tax assessed value—can be appealed for possibly huge savings.

This notion of potential hidden income in property taxes first occurred to me in 2011 when the commercial real estate market in my area (the Greater Triangle Area of North Carolina) was suffering from the Great Recession. A property owner retained my brokerage firm to list their restaurant building that was in foreclosure. The owner wanted to list the property for sale at $750,000. With a tax assessed value of $1,500,000, there was little interest in the property. My primary marketing strategy for the property was that the high tax value was a perceived, built-in value in the property (i.e. if someone purchased the property for $750,000, the value was actually $1,500,000).

After achieving very little traction with this sales opportunity, it occurred to me that the property owner was paying over $17,000 a year in property taxes based on assessed value, which was significantly higher than the true market value of the property. Faced with this obstacle to the sale of the property, I envisioned a new value proposition for my client. I offered to formally appeal the property tax value with the local municipality, free of charge!

We agreed that if I was successful with the appeal—meaning the local municipality agreed to reduce the assessed value of the property thus netting tax savings to the property owner—I would earn 50% of the first year tax savings. If I was unsuccessful—meaning the local municipality maintained the property value "as-is" and the property owner saved nothing—I would earn nothing.

It seemed like a very easy decision for this owner and many, many owners after him, since there is no downside to the property owner. If we do nothing, he will have to pay $17,000 in taxes at the end of the year. Whatever I can potentially save him is pure profit and savings, and it does not cost him anything upfront.

In this case, the successful appeal reduced the tax value over 50% to under $700,000. This reduced the annual tax bill to a little over $8,000 a year, more than a 50% reduction from the $17,000 tax bill that he was accustomed to paying and that he would have paid that year if we did not appeal. The annual savings to this owner were over $9,000, and my fee was 50% of the first year savings, or approximately $4,500.

Tax Value Before Appeal	$1,477,000
Tax Bill Before Appeal	-$17,000
Tax Value After Appeal	$687,000
Tax Bill After Appeal	-$8,000
Annual Cash Savings	$70,000
Compound Effect on NOI & Cashflow Boost	**$9,000**
Market CAP Rate for Asset Type	7.50%
Instant Equity Gain	**$120,000**

The entire appeal took me less than four hours to complete from start to finish, including time I spent making the first sales pitch to the property owner, time writing an essay to the county's Assessor's Office justifying why the tax assessed value should be less than what was reported, time babysitting negotiations with the county throughout the appeal process, and time submitting a final invoice. The deal in its entirety took approximately three to four months from appeal submission date to the Assessor's Office issuing their decision on reduced value, after which I collected on the invoice.

While one can look at tax appeals as a secondary revenue stream or even as a stand-alone, full-time business, like I did in my old firm at the time, the importance of tax appeals to the property owners is much more. In the case of this property owner, their first-year tax savings were $4,500 on their tax bill, but ongoing savings for remaining years were $9,000 annually. Not only does minimizing operating expenses such as property taxes help carry properties, but these reductions in property tax bills also result in a proportionate increase in NOI for the property.

As we know, commercial properties are valued by a function of NOI the property generates; the higher the NOI the more the property is worth. So, if the subject property was occupied with any amount of rental income, an annual savings of $9,000 on taxes and consequently an annual increase of NOI by $9,000 would result in a value increase of anywhere from $112,500-$150,000, assuming the market capitalization rate (CAP rate) for such an asset in that area is between 6% and 8%.

It is even more important to appeal property taxes on land since land typically generates no revenue. Without an income stream land becomes very expensive and especially cumbersome to carry long term, even if it is paid for and does not have a mortgage.

I remember one parcel of land on which we appealed the tax value in the Charlotte, NC area. It was approximately 130 acres, zoned industrial, and assessed at approximately $6,900,000. With an annual tax bill of $88,000, $7,333 each month is a lot of money to pay in property taxes on a piece of property that generates no income.

Offering our property tax appeal services to the property owner was an easy value proposition. In this case, we were successful in proving that the land was a former manufacturing site and had some contamination. The local municipality agreed to reduce the tax value on the land to $1,400,000, which reduced the annual tax bill to $18,000. That's over $70,000 a year back into the property owner's pocket instead of giving it to the county. That is more than the average American earns in a year.

Tax Value Before Appeal	$6,900,000
Tax Bill Before Appeal	$88,000
Tax Value After Appeal	$1,400,000
Tax Bill After Appeal	$18,000
Annual Cash Savings	$70,000
Extra Cash to Stay in Your Pocket	**$5,833/mo**

After I completed a few appeals myself, I developed a two-page list of potential ways to justify cases to a local taxing authority when evaluating two properties side by side. I could argue why one should be assessed for half of the other's assessed value. Right-of-way give-aways, deed restrictions, non-conforming parking ratios, ingress and egress issues, visibility issues, powerline easements, and flood zones are all valid and successfully tested arguments to justify revisions of a property tax assessment.

It started with that one small property back in 2011, and over 1,000 appeals later, it has turned into a full-blown division of my old company. Our nationwide operation represented some of the largest publicly traded real estate firms in the United States, performing tax appeals on commercial buildings throughout the East Coast.

For example, we represented the owner of a regional shopping mall in the Triangle NC area with a tax-assessed value of $175,000,000. After our successful tax appeal, the tax value was reduced to $146,000,000, saving the owner nearly $300,000 a year in property taxes. Aside from the cash savings on an annual basis, these savings boosted NOI, resulting in an over $4 million gain in value at a 6.75% capitalization rate.

Tax Value Before Appeal	$175,148,299
Tax Bill Before Appeal	$1,784,409
Tax Value After Appeal	$146,479,439
Tax Bill After Appeal	$1,492,331
Annual Cash Savings	$292,078
Annual NOI & Cash Flow Boost	**$292,078**
Market CAP Rate for Asset Type	6.75%
Instant Equity Gain	**$4,327,081**

While tax appeals can be a great business, over the years I have learned that it's best to focus on the one thing that makes you the most money and not diversify into so many silos that you lose focus in your core business. In other words, my advice is simple—find the best way to make money and do not deviate from it.

So when we started Cityplat in 2019, we deliberately chose to not offer tax appeal services to outside clients so that we could focus on the one thing that has created the most amount of wealth for me and my partners—the acquisition of value-add, small-bay industrial and neighborhood retail centers. We still do tax appeals every year on all our assets to optimize NOI and maximize equity gain; we just no longer offer it to third-party clients as a service.

EXAMPLES OF TAX APPEALS

People tend to think that the property tax assessed value directly correlates with the true property value. However, as you can see from examples in this chapter, the property tax value has a relationship of inverse correlation with the actual property value. At least on income-producing properties, the lower the tax value, the lower the operating expenses, and the higher the net operating income, the higher the property's market value.

Below are some more examples of the earlier tax appeals we completed on various property types that clearly illustrate this inverse relationship, as you can see from the summary of NOI savings on these particular properties.

Medical Office Building, Raleigh, NC

Tax Value Before Appeal	$5,402,237
Tax Bill Before Appeal	$49,187
Tax Value After Appeal	$3,279,679
Tax Bill After Appeal	$29,925
Annual Cash Savings	$19,262
Annual NOI & Cash Flow Boost	**$19,262**
Market CAP Rate for Asset Type	5.50%
Instant Equity Gain	**$350,218**

Traditional Office Building, Raleigh, NC

Tax Value Before Appeal	$26,385,877
Tax Bill Before Appeal	$273,226
Tax Value After Appeal	$20,337,098
Tax Bill After Appeal	$210,591
Annual Cash Savings	$62,635
Annual NOI & Cash Flow Boost	**$62,635**
Market CAP Rate for Asset Type	6.00%
Instant Equity Gain	**$1,043,917**

Typical Freestanding Retail, Raleigh, NC

Tax Value Before Appeal	$4,359,535
Tax Bill Before Appeal	$39,563
Tax Value After Appeal	$2,599,618
Tax Bill After Appeal	$23,592
Annual Cash Savings	$15,971
Annual NOI & Cash Flow Boost	**$15,971**
Market CAP Rate for Asset Type	6.25%
Instant Equity Gain	**$255,536**

Typical Retail Mall, Cary, NC

Tax Value Before Appeal	$64,076,917
Tax Bill Before Appeal	$609,052
Tax Value After Appeal	$57,582,664
Tax Bill After Appeal	$547,324
Annual Cash Savings	$61,728
Annual NOI & Cash Flow Boost	**$61,728**
Market CAP Rate for Asset Type	**7.75%**
Instant Equity Gain	**$796,490**

Typical Hotel, RTP, NC

Tax Value Before Appeal	$13,713,366
Tax Bill Before Appeal	$189,832
Tax Value After Appeal	$10,392,519
Tax Bill After Appeal	$143,862
Annual Cash Savings	$45,970
Annual NOI & Cash Flow Boost	**$45,970**
Market CAP Rate for Asset Type	6.00%
Instant Equity Gain	**$766,166**

POSSIBLE REASONS TO JUSTIFY A PROPERTY TAX ASSESSED VALUE REDUCTION

A tax appeal is basically when you take a blank sheet of paper and write an essay, as short or long as you can, justifying all possible reasons why the assessed value for a particular property should be lower.

The first and most obvious place to look for reasons for a reduction in assessed value is the county tax records. Determine if there are inconsistencies between the county records and what actually exists on your property. Most property tax assessor's offices complete mass assessment on properties and do not individually review each property. Oftentimes, the input data used to establish value includes errors and incorrect information.

An example could be the incorrect tax or millage rate applied to the property and used to calculate the tax bill. Less obvious inconsistencies might include incorrect square footage on record with the county or incorrect classification of the asset. In the case of incorrect classification, an office building may be classified as medical office space, which is assessed at a higher rate than traditional office space, or warehouse space may be classified as flex space which is usually assessed at a higher rate than warehouse space.

In our tax appeals we have developed and used every possible reason why two properties side by side may have a different tax value. Start your tax appeal by reviewing the property valuation using the three common ways most appraisers, banks, and insurance companies value a property—the income approach to value, sales comparison approach, and replacement cost approach. These are the most obvious and easily argued reasons to justify a tax reduction.

INCOME APPROACH TO VALUE

If the property is income producing, simply identify the net operating income of the property, divide it by the market CAP rate, and compare the value you come up with to the value assigned by the Assessor's Office. Ideally you want to have at least two or three years of prior income and expense statements to establish the property income performance history. If your resulting value is less than the assessed value, this is a strong component of your tax appeal because CAP rate valuations are not subjective and little can be argued against such valuations. Conversely, if your value is equal to or greater than the assessed value, do not use this approach as part of your argument and instead consider the sales comparison approach and replacement cost approach.

SALES COMPARISON APPROACH

Determine the price at which other similar properties, ideally three to five similar properties, most recently sold in the area.

Similarities would include office to office, retail to retail, or land to land of similar size, shape, use, zoning, etc. Calculate the price on a per-square-foot basis and arrive at an average cost per square foot. Calculate how your property would be valued by using the price per square foot average. If your value is less than your property's assessed value, then you have a very good justification for a tax value reduction because the sales comparison approach leaves little to no room for subjective interpretation. If the value you come up with is higher than the current tax value, simply do not use this reasoning among your arguments.

REPLACEMENT COST APPROACH

This approach is primarily used by insurance companies to value properties. Most likely, this approach would not be helpful if you are evaluating older properties. The replacement cost approach is literally what it will cost to replace the exact property in its exact location in the event it is destroyed by a fire or a natural disaster. Since the price of new construction today is probably much higher than it was when an older property was built, this strategy is not recommended when appealing older buildings. If, however, your subject property is a fairly new property, then replacement cost may likely be lower than the value assigned by the tax assessor's office.

ALTERNATIVE FACTORS

Other potential points of argument can include everything from ingress/egress issues, non-conforming parking ratios, visibility issues, future right-of-way dedications, non-conforming zoning, deed restrictions, easements, flood plains, proximity to railroads, functional obsolescence, or other factors that may adversely affect and diminish the value of the property.

The same factors can have a positive effect on some properties while having a diminishing value effect on others. A railroad spur that backs up to an industrial or manufacturing facility can have a positive impact on a property, but the same railroad spur backing up to a residential apartment property will have a major negative effect on the property. So you should use common sense when determining which factors and reasons will most effectively justify a tax appeal for the particular property under analysis.

Successful factors used to justify tax reduction can include very logical factors, such as comparable sales, net operating income, and other factors based on pure math. Likewise, very subjective arguments, such as bad publicity or negative stigma associated with the property, can be quite effective.

In one case of a shopping mall appeal, we documented negative publicity associated with recent crime activity that took place at the property. The discomfort generated by the negative publicity resulted in a decline in visitors to the shopping mall and a significant decline in sales for retailers and tenants at that mall.

Crime reports and vandalism would probably not have a long-term effect on the sale price of a Class A retail mall asset; nevertheless, we were successfully able to argue that such declines in revenue would ultimately drive down the lease rates on retail spaces at the shopping mall and affect the property's NOI, a critical factor in the valuation of income-producing properties.

HISTORIC LANDMARK DESIGNATION

Properties with historic landmark designations benefit from a 50% property tax waiver in most municipalities. For example, a property is valued at $1,000,000 with an annual tax bill of $12,000 per year. If the property could obtain a historic landmark designation, the property owner would only pay 50% of the property taxes owed. In this example, there would be a $6,000 annual savings on taxes, translating to extra income added to the bottom line NOI. Assuming a 6.00% CAP rate, these savings would result in a net increase in value of $100,000 and equate to $100,000 in extra equity.

A common misperception is that a property or building must be old to be eligible for a historic landmark designation. Any building, even one that was recently constructed, is eligible for a historic landmark designation if it can be classified as a "contributing structure" to the historic, cultural, aesthetic, or architectural significance of the community. A building can be brand new, but if it can be argued that the building carries an architectural or cultural significance to the surrounding neighborhood, it can achieve a landmark designation and benefit from tax savings. I have friends who successfully achieved historic landmark designations for an all-glass, Class A office high-rise building for significant savings.

The bigger the property, the bigger the potential savings. The bigger the NOI, the bigger the equity increase in the property through obtaining such designation. For example, a high-rise office building in the downtown sector of an average American city valued at $30,000,000 may have a tax bill of $360,000 a year. A historic designation for the building would result in a benefit of $180,000 in annual savings, both in operating expenses and an NOI boost for such a building. This type of NOI increase will result in a $3,000,000 gain in value by the simple recording of paperwork designating the building as unique and contributing to the community.

One of my good friends and mentors owns a multi-tenant high-rise office building in downtown Raleigh. This 150,000 square foot, Class A, 15-story office tower had a tax assessed value of $35,008,826 as of the January 2025 tax assessment year. Normal property taxes on this building would have been $327,858 per year.

Several years prior, my friend successfully achieved historic landmark designation for his property, reducing the property taxes by half, down to $163,929. The building's market CAP rate as of the date of this publication is approximately 7.00%. Applying the 7.00% CAP rate to this example translates into a value increase of $2,341,843 if my friend were to sell this building on an open market.

Tax Value Before & After	$35,008,826
Tax Bill Before Landmark Designation	$327,858
Tax Bill After Landmark Designation	$163,929
Annual NOI & Cash Flow Boost	$163,929
Market CAP Rate for Asset Type	7.00%
Instant Equity Gain	**$2,341,843**

The downside of obtaining a historic landmark designation on a building is that if it was ever redeveloped in the future, it would trigger a repayment of some or all of the deferred taxes. That is why it makes sense to obtain historic designation only on buildings that are unlikely to be redeveloped in the foreseeable future for higher and better use.

2

Vending, Laundry, & ATMs

> "Maximizing your revenue per square foot of usable space makes all the difference to your bottom line results."

AUTOMATIC TELLER MACHINES

Nearly every type of property has an area of 24 square feet that can be carved out with minor modification and without much harm to the use of the property. If you own a property that has any kind of commercial frontage or is located in a heavily trafficked pedestrian area, you should seriously consider creating space for an ATM on your property.

An average ATM space will typically lease for $500-$1,400 per month and require an area of approximately 4' x 6'. Calculated on a per-square-foot basis, that is at least $6,000 annual income for 24 square feet (or $250 per square foot). Since most ATM space is leased to a bank or credible financial institution, that lease would likely be valued at a very low CAP rate, possibly 5% or as low as 4% depending on the length of the lease term. At a 5% CAP rate, that would result in a $120,000 increase in property value. In high-demand areas with heavy pedestrian traffic, an ATM lease could bring in $1,200-$1,400 per month, translating to an equity increase of up to $420,000 for a simple lease of otherwise unusable area.

Added Monthly Rent from ATM Lease	$1,200
Annual NOI & Cash Flow Boost	**$14,400**
Market CAP Rate for Asset Type	4.00%
Instant Equity Gain	**$360,000**

A property owner may also choose to install an ATM on their own and collect ATM fees on cash withdrawals, but such an operation requires more hands-on management and weekly attendance to load up the ATM with cash, etc.

VENDING MACHINES IN APARTMENT BUILDINGS OR OFFICE BUILDINGS

Vending machines placed in high-traffic areas of your property can add a surprising amount of cash flow to your bottom line. Vending machine inventories can be customized to suit the needs of your tenant base and could include any variety of items such as snacks, drinks, cold sandwiches, hot coffee, tea, or incidentals. Your imagination is the limit on what can be sold. The type of machine will depend on what products you intend to offer. Machines with card readers are more desirable to consumers who are less likely to carry cash or coins. It is also easier to track income and profit with credit and debit purchases than with strictly cash options.

If you choose to purchase or lease the machines, there are many reputable vendors offering state-of-the-art equipment with favorable pricing and terms. Consumers are more likely to be attracted to newer, more automated machines. In this regard, a lease could enable you to upgrade at regular time intervals. Vending machine leases can also include a $1 buyout of equipment at the end of their term. At the time of this publication, the purchase of a combination drink/snack vending machine with a card reader could be anywhere between $2,000 and $5,000. Monthly lease rates can begin at around $50 per month and range upwards of $150 per month and may include a security deposit and/or down payment. Additional costs include the products to keep the machines stocked.

It is difficult to estimate the total cost and profit because it depends entirely on what kind of products you choose and how often the machines are used. However, for most common product items typically seen in vending machines, such as snacks and soft drinks, you can reasonably expect a 50% profit margin. With an average of 10 items sold per day, you would realize approximately 300 items sold per month at an average profit of $1.00.

The below calculation shows how the math works out on adding a vending component to your existing real estate that has a high-traffic common area, where a vending machine could be placed. This calculation assumes adding the two most common machines, one for snacks and one for soft drinks.

Average Price Per Vending Item	$2.00
Average Profit Per Vending Item (50% Margin)	$1.00
Average Number of Vending Items Sold per Month	300
Monthly Profit off Vending Sales	+$300/mo
Cost of Leasing Vending Machines	-$100/mo
Annual NOI & Cash Flow Boost ($200/mo)	**$2,400/mo**
Market CAP Rate for Asset Type	7.50%
Instant Equity Gain	**$32,000**

Vending machines require hands-on management and weekly attendance to load up machines with products, etc. But if you or your staff already have weekly attendance to your building on your calendar for other maintenance items, such as janitorial, adding the stocking of vending machines to that list will hardly require any additional time.

Another option would be to allow third-party vendors to lease space in your property, rather than renting or purchasing, stocking, and servicing vending machines. However, a hands-on owner who does not mind spending time managing the inventory can definitely benefit from installing his or her own vending machines at their property.

COIN-OPERATED LAUNDRIES

Today most new construction of housing units includes washer and dryer connections. However, in an urban setting with a lot of older properties around, many apartment buildings were not built with washer and dryer connections in each housing unit. This construction neglect in older apartment buildings presents an opportunity for the owner of such properties to potentially convert ancillary or otherwise unutilized space in the building (such as a basement) into a coin-operated laundry facility.

Utilizing ancillary space in apartment buildings can be a great way to add NOI to your bottom line. In high-demand markets, such new found NOI translates to huge equity gains with minimum out-of-pocket cost.

To illustrate this concept, I will use one laundry facility that I built out of the non-existent basement of an old apartment building I owned in downtown Raleigh. The apartment building was a 24-unit historic apartment building close to NC State University. Most residents in the building were students upgrading from a dormitory to an individual apartment. So I knew that most of my residents would be accustomed to using public laundry facilities to do their laundry.

This particular building had a small, dirt crawl space in one portion of the building that a person could barely crawl into. When renovating the building, I decided to have the construction crews dig out the crawl space and add a full-size laundry room with 9' ceilings and a handicap ramp for accessibility per ADA code. The newly constructed basement was just big enough to accommodate four coin-operated washing machines and four coin-operated dryers (as well as a few vending machines, of course, for supplemental income).

Remember, I had 24 units in the building, most of which were two-bedroom units. This meant that two or more people resided in each unit, so there were approximately 48 residents who would need to do laundry on a weekly basis. With each resident doing two loads of laundry each week—at an average cost of $1.50 per wash and per dry—adding this simple laundry room meant an average revenue of $6 per resident per week for two loads of clothing to wash and dry. That meant each resident would spend, on average, $26 per month on laundry, which generates $1,248 of extra income per month.

As with all my investment properties, this property was located in a high-demand, low cap-rate location. The extra $14,976 per year in NOI meant an instant equity gain of $249,600, assuming a 6.00% CAP rate. Not a bad return on an investment of less than $50,000. Again, this is a very simple and humble example of what four washers and dryers can mean to you in an apartment building. The larger your property, the greater the effect these numbers will have on your equity position and cash flow.

Average Profit Per Load	$1.50
Total Residents in the Building	48
Approximate Loads per month	832
Annual NOI & Cash Flow Boost	**$14,976**
Market CAP Rate for Asset Type	6.00%
Instant Equity Gain	**$249,600**

These numbers might be slightly offset by some added utility expenses but are representative of the returns that can be realized from this type of investment. It has been about a decade since I did this project, and I have since sold the building. These numbers are approximate based on what I recollect from when I did it as a kid at the beginning of my path in real estate entrepreneurship.

Nevertheless, in high-demand locations, every $100 of found rental income per month translates into tens of thousands of dollars of new equity. Awareness of this fact can lead to recognizing opportunities where you have previously failed to see an opportunity.

Early in my investing career, I went to the neighborhoods that had a lot of low-income housing that I couldn't buy or didn't want to buy. But, while I did not necessarily care to own the real estate in those particular locations, I saw a need for a laundry facility to service all those low-income housing complexes. So, you can bet that aside from my real estate investments, I ended up owning and operating laundromats in those locations with as many as 30 to 40 machines as a weekend business.

Those laundromats required less than 15 minutes a week of my time. I would swing by on Friday night before going to dinner and pick up the cash from the coin dispensers. They cash flowed like cash cows for me! Real estate usually takes a long time to see profits that you can spend on personal needs, but laundromats spat out cash every week that I could touch. It felt like instant gratification, and I loved it.

3

PARKING

"I never had a parking lot tenant complain that they have a leaky roof or stained carpet."

PARKING

I cannot tell you how many apartment, retail, and office buildings I have seen in urban settings with parking lots that are being offered free of charge to the tenants on a first-come, first-served basis. I know you can already see where I am going with this. Similar to other topics described in this chapter, parking lots can be a potential gold mine to create extra cash flow and equity in your existing buildings.

I have purchased many apartment and office buildings in high-density locations with parking lots to service those buildings that were not generating any revenue. In high-price-per-square-foot land locations, it is a shame to not fully maximize revenue from every square foot of the property.

Many property owners do not pay attention to this potential revenue stream because they think "Oh, what could $100 per month in parking rent possibly do for me? It's more of a hassle, than it's worth." Well, those owners clearly do not understand the concepts of leverageable equity, compounding NOI, and CAP rate compression in high-demand locations. Because if they did, they would quickly recognize that a $100 per month rent from a parking space translates to approximately $20,000 of new found equity at a 6.00% CAP rate. What if your apartment building had 27 extra spaces that were available on a first-come, first-served basis and not generating revenue? Do you see how much difference a silly $100 per month parking space could make in your net worth?

Also, unlike buildings, I have never had a surface level parking lot that had a leak, or needed carpet replacement, or had clogged plumbing, or had malfunctioning air conditioning, or had bad odors. I am being sarcastic here, but what I mean by this is that parking lots are in general very low maintenance. I would prefer parking lot tenants all day long over Class A apartment or office building tenants.

Consider the following examples of a few buildings I purchased that came with extra parking lots, which will illustrate my point.

Below is a church building that I purchased near NC State University a number of years ago for $860,000. The building is 6,000 square feet and sits on 0.21 acres of high-density zoned land. It's a corner lot, too. I purchased it for land value with the intent to demolish the building and build a 5-story mixed-use building, like I have done on other blocks of that street.

The building came with an underground parking garage of 21 spaces. With a lot of retail businesses and housing units around and limited parking on the street, parking is a scarce commodity in this area. Construction drawings for redevelopment of the site for intended use in my city can take up to several years, especially if it relates to a strategic location surrounded by highly vocal neighborhood residents. So renting out parking spaces could be an easy and great way to generate revenue to pay for property taxes and carrying costs on an empty building.

With 21 spaces rented to nearby businesses for employee parking at $150 per month per space, this parking lot generates $3,150 per month in revenue. That is approximately 70% of my mortgage payment on the building, which makes carrying the building long-term while working on construction plans much more affordable at a $1,350 per month cost vs. $4,500 per month. But if we were to keep the building as a rental property and not redevelop it, the extra $3,150 per month income, or $37,800 per year in extra NOI, translates into $630,000 of extra equity in the building at a 6.0% CAP rate, which is a market CAP rate for this type of asset in this particular location.

Covered Parking Spaces	21
Monthly Rent per Park	$150
Total Monthly Revenue from Parking	$3,150
Annual NOI & Cash Flow Boost	**$37,800**
Market CAP Rate for Asset Type	6.00%
Instant Equity Gain	**$630,000**

That is three quarters of the total $860,000 price I paid for the property, which also came with a 6,000 square foot building rentable for office or retail use at a minimum of $24 per square foot on the open market. If I were able to increase parking rents by another $50 per month (with time, I am sure I will be able to do so), then parking income alone would pay for the entire property ($200/space x 21 spaces x 12 months = $50,400/year @ 6.0% CAP = $840,000). So much for giving no considerations to $150/mo parking spaces as is the case with so many property owners!

Here is another example of an apartment building that I purchased some time ago in the downtown area of my city. It is an 11-unit historic apartment building—one of the very first apartment buildings built in Raleigh.

The building came with a small parking lot with seven parking spaces that were on a first-come, first-served basis for the residents. The building is a block away from the state capitol and the Governor's Mansion. It is surrounded for several blocks by state, county, and city offices. It is only a few blocks away from numerous coffee shops, restaurants, and nightlife venues, and two major colleges are within a few blocks, too. It is in an absolutely phenomenal and irreplaceable location. It's a 12 on a location scale of 1 to 10. So, even if none of my 11 tenants want to pay for off-street parking at $75 per month, I have a lot of people around me that would gladly pay a nominal rent of $75 per month for an off-street parking space. Seven spaces at $75 per month is $6,300 per year in extra revenue.

With a market CAP rate of 5.5% for such an asset type, this is an instant gain of equity of $114,545. Not much, given the purchase price I paid for the building of $1,950,000.

Surface Parking Spaces	7
Monthly Rent per Park	$75
Total Monthly Revenue from Parking	$525
Annual NOI & Cash Flow Boost	**$6,300**
Market CAP Rate for Asset Type	5.50%
Instant Equity Gain	**$114,545**

Again, a $114,545 gain is nothing to brag about. But it's all relative, and every little bit counts. Also, keep in mind that this is $114,545 of equity that took about a week to create by running a few ads for parking for rent.

As described in earlier chapters, you can be assured that an application for landmark designation as well as installation of coin-operated laundry facilities are also underway for this building. In low-cap-rate markets, you should exploit every tool available to you to maximize NOI and create new leverageable equity, as over time these small changes will make you millions of dollars.

Here is another historic apartment building I purchased in Raleigh that came not with one but with two extra parking lots.

I paid $2.6 million for this 15-unit apartment building over three retail units. The property came with two parking lots across the street consisting of 15 spaces and 27 spaces respectively.

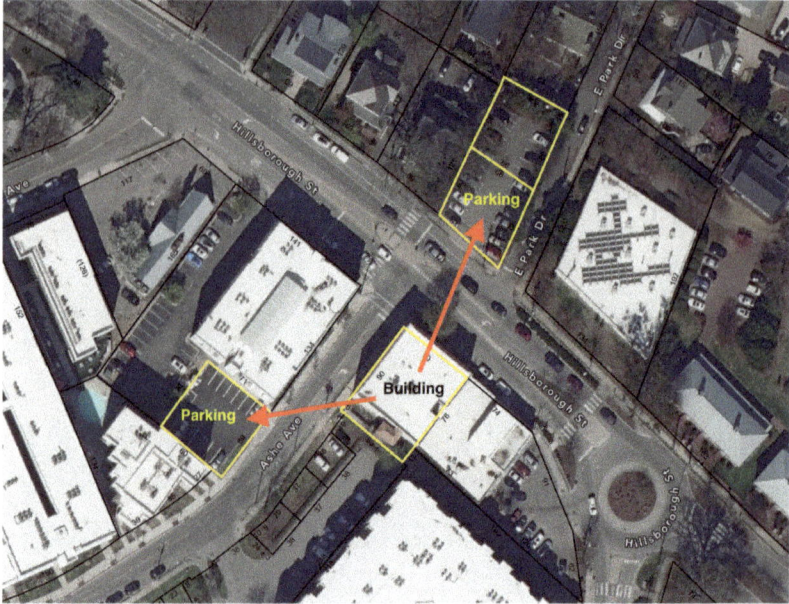

The apartment building had an NOI of approximately $80,000 per year at the time of purchase, and parking lots were free of charge to tenants. I renovated the apartments, added digitally operated laundry that direct deposits cash to my checking account, and increased overall NOI to approximately $280,000. With increased NOI, the investment started to make sense.

But then I turned my attention to the parking lots. Instead of trying to self-manage the parking lots and trying to find 42 tenants myself, I hired a parking company to manage and operate the parking lots on my behalf based on an 80/20 revenue share, with 80% going to me as landowner. They would handle leasing the spaces on a monthly and hourly basis, enforce violators, maintain the property, and collect late fees.

Unlike in earlier examples, with this property I transitioned to not having to collect many small checks from many different tenants myself. Instead I just deal with one company that manages it for me and sends me 80% of the total revenue at the end of each month. I found that the extra income they are able to generate through professional and efficient management far exceeds the 20% I'm giving up as a management fee. In this particular case, the net parking revenue to me from these two parking lots averages $3,200 and $4,300, respectively ($90,000 per year), which is more than the original NOI from the entire apartment building originally! The value of these two parking lots is now around $1,800,000 based on a 5.00% CAP on income, which covers more than half of my original purchase price for the building.

Not to keep beating a dead horse, but I would like to share one more example to drive the point home on the power of parking lots.

Right in the middle of the COVID-19 pandemic in 2020, I purchased this 0.27 lot in the downtown of my city with plans to develop a 12-story hotel here or to sell on a longterm ground lease to a developer upon entitlements.

The pandemic had a very adverse effect on the hospitality industry. Unfortunately, shortly after the purchase, the
development of the hotel on the site become non-viable for
the foreseeable future due to financing difficulties and project
economics. Our acquisition cost of this quarter-acre parcel
was $1,700,000, so we had to figure out a way to carry the site
for several years until redevelopment was going to become
viable again. So I had no better option but to turn this site into
a gravel parking lot with the hope of generating some revenue
to help pay for the taxes and mortgage on $1.7 million.

Since this site was located in a business area surrounded
by retail and offices and not in a residential area, renting the
parking spaces on monthly accounts to residents in the area
like I have done previously on other lots was not viable here.
So I decided to hire a parking management company to man-

age and operate the parking lot on our behalf and rent spaces on an hourly basis instead of monthly contracts. The results exceeded all of our expectations. The parking lot happened to be across the street from a popular breakfast café and coffee shop that captured morning traffic and across the street from a popular brewery that captured evening traffic. So the parking lot stayed packed with cars around the clock.

With modern technology, the management company was able to see peak hours and adjust the hourly and weekend rates accordingly for maximum revenue. They were also able to install automated cameras on site that would match license plates against a database to automate a non-payment charge for violators who did not pay to park.

Based on my previous experience with parking lots, I expected this 0.27-acre parking lot to generate around $2500-$3000/mo if we did a good job managing it effectively. Working with a good parking operator, we exceeded our expectations as we averaged a revenue of $12,000-$15,000 per month.

After a couple of months of this, the parking company gave us a recommendation and an industry insight that if we installed lighting and paved the parking lot, the parking lot would appeal more to female customers who would feel safer parking there. That would tremendously drive our revenue up based on their experience. We followed their recommendations and paved the parking lot and added lighting and cameras on site.

Total upgrades cost us $27,000, but the very next month, our revenue jumped to $20,000 per month. We have been averaging $20,000-$25,000 per month ever since. Who would have thought that this silly little 0.27-acre parking lot can generate such tremendous rental income if managed correctly? Now it not only has enough revenue to cover the debt service and carrying costs, it produces enough positive cash flow that we can hold on to it indefinitely without a need to redevelop a hotel building here. Leasing parking lots is an excellent way to effectuate a covered land play in an urban setting.

4

ROOF TOP & CELL TOWERS

"Urban roof tops are a
grossly under-utilized
commodity that can be a great
source of income."

ROOFTOP LEASES

A roof is defined by Merriman-Webster as "the cover of a
building." Built to withstand harsh weather conditions, a roof is
also a potential hidden income opportunity. Leasing a rooftop
area for a wireless (or cell) tower is another hidden income
source in your building. A cell tower requires as little as 50
square feet for installation, so the size of your roof is not
necessarily an obstacle to pursuing this additional revenue
source. One cell tower or rooftop lease could support as many
as five carriers and as many as 15 other types of antennas, such
as GPS relays, cable, etc. As of the date of this publication, a
typical cell carrier would pay up to $2,000 in monthly rent;

other types of smaller antennas would bring in $200-$300 in rent per month. So, on a single cell tower or rooftop lease, you can generate up to $12,000-$15,000 gross revenue per month. If you are on a 50/50 split with the supplier/installer, you can generate net income for yourself of up to $6,000-$7,000 per month. Once the tower and lease are in place, they tend to stay for a very long time. Consequently, income from such leases is perceived as very low risk and tends to trade at low cap rates, 4.00-5.00%. A $72,000-$84,000 NOI per year would result in an equity/value increase for your property of $1.4M-$2.1M with minimal to no out-of-pocket cost.

Added Monthly Revenue from Roof Top Lease	$7,000
Annual NOI & Cash Flow Boost	**$84,000**

Market CAP Rate for Asset Type	4.50%
Instant Equity Gain	**$1,866,667**

UP FRONT INFRASTRUCTURE COSTS

You can either pay for the infrastructure and secure the lease with carriers yourself to maintain 100% of the revenue or outsource the expense and negotiation work to companies that do it professionally. The installation of equipment can be costly and would require specialty engineering services. You may also find it challenging to establish contact with wireless carriers or even to receive a return call. I recommend deferring the infrastructure work and lease negotiations to professionals. There are several major players in this arena that control the majority of wireless tower and rooftop leases. SBA, Crown Castle, and American Tower are some of the largest in the country, but there are many others that have relationships with wireless carriers.

My experience is that working with tower companies results in a much more time-efficient and cost-effective lease. They typically pay for infrastructure themselves, secure leases through their established relationships, and split revenues with the property owner on a 50/50 split, or sometimes even better. I have been able to secure 70/30 splits (with 70% going to me as property owner) in the past with no upfront investment on my part.

FREESTANDING CELL TOWERS

Not all property owners have the luxury of owning mid-rise or high-rise buildings with flat roofs in an urban setting to be able to capitalize on the rooftops of their buildings. However, owning suburban properties still presents an opportunity to get your small piece of a multi-billion dollar telecommunications industry.

Suburban properties of most types are usually spread over large areas of land. In nearly all suburban developed properties I have seen, there is a 100' by 100' space that can be found where a cell tower can be placed. 100' by 100' is the preferred size for cell tower providers looking to lease land for cell tower installation to allow space for servicing; however, I have seen some on footprints as small as 50' and 50'. Ultimately the dimensions, location, and zoning of the plot of land allocated for cell towers will be dictated by your local city or county ordinances.

If you can carve out a 5,000-10,000 square foot section on your property, a cell tower can be accommodated for extra income—possibly even more income than you are currently realizing from the building on your property. Although income from traditional cell towers can be similar to that described in the previous section on rooftop leases, the supporting infrastructure on traditional cell towers is more complex than rooftops and thus much more costly to install (can be upwards of $250,000). Traditional cell towers are also much more visible from the street and can possibly take away from the overall curb appeal of your property. Nevertheless, if you stay emotionally detached from properties and the bottom line to your pocketbook is the ultimate decision factor for you, there is little difference in potential revenue from traditional cell towers versus rooftop leases.

If your focus is to maximize revenue and equity in your properties and to build wealth, I would recommend you carefully analyze your real estate portfolio to explore opportunities where cell towers can be installed. The need for cell tower installation by carriers in a particular area ultimately depends on how many people the cell tower will service. Considering that a suburban setting usually means a less densely populated area than a city center, rental income or profit sharing that carriers are willing to pay for a traditional cell tower may vary. A cell tower in a less densely populated area may generate $3,000 per month, whereas one in a densely populated area may generate $7,000-$8,000 per month in income to the property owner, as described in a previous section. For illustration purposes, let's analyze a cell tower with a $3,000 per month income in a suburban setting to see what effect it will have on your equity position.

Added Monthly Revenue from Suburban Cell Tower	$3,000
Annual NOI & Cash Flow Boost	**$36,000**
Market CAP Rate for Asset Type	4.50%
Instant Equity Gain	**$800,000**

As you can see from the above analysis, even a nominal income from a suburban cell tower lease can have a major impact on your equity position. Such equity gain can then be recapitalized in the event of a sale and represents approximately 20 years of an average American's salary before taxes. That's the beauty of demand real estate—small changes to cash flow create huge differences in one's net worth.

5

BILLBOARDS

"Sometimes miscellaneous factors in a property have more value than the property itself."

BILLBOARDS

Traditional, outdoor billboards have been a significant advertising component for literally hundreds of years. The 1900s were considered their golden age, especially after the invention of the automobile. Since the passage of the Highway Beautification Act of 1965, there has been a nationwide effort to curtail billboard advertising. Consequently, it is extremely hard to obtain permitting for a new billboard.

However, there are plenty of properties with billboards already in place, with minimum rent. When buying these properties, buyers and sellers rarely assign much value to billboards as they are typically leased for a minimum rent of $200-$500 per month. The reality is that billboards are much more valuable and can generate significantly higher revenues.

A number of years ago, I represented a client in the purchase of a small strip shopping center in Raleigh. Four tenants were paying $3,000-$4,000 each on a triple-net basis. On the property, there was a billboard with a month-to-month lease paying $250 in rent. No value had been assigned to the billboard income when determining the sales price of $1,700,000 for the subject property. The property is located on a major thoroughfare in Raleigh, with over 60,000 vehicles passing by every day.

I was familiar with the location. A few years prior to my client's purchase, I rented this particular billboard along with eight others on that thoroughfare as advertisement for various divisions of my company. At that time, we paid over $4,000 per month for just one side of the billboard! And that was a discounted rate since we negotiated a rental package of eight billboards with a prepaid 12-month contract.

Shortly after closing, my client advised me that he was considering increasing the billboard rent to $400 or $500 per month, up from the $250 they were currently paying. I advised my client that he would be out of his mind if he charged them anything less than $3,000-$4,000 per month or 50% of the revenue split. My client hesitated to believe that $3,000-$4,000 per month was possible and thought the billboard advertising company might terminate the lease and move the billboard.

I told him that a) it would be a $250,000 upfront investment for them to install a billboard elsewhere; b) the billboard was an established income stream for the billboard advertising company, as they can generate $9,000 in monthly revenue from advertisements on both sides of the billboard; and c) it is virtually impossible to obtain permitting for a new billboard. I was confident they would not go anywhere. I convinced my client to try this strategy and see what their response was when he quoted them $4,000 monthly rent, up from their current rate of $250 per month.

When the sales representative from the billboard advertising company called my client to talk about their lease renewal, my client told him that he was thinking $4,500 to $5,000 monthly rent to leave room for negotiation. The sales representative burst out laughing on the phone to my client. Well, it actually infuriated my client that someone had such disrespect for him that they laughed in his face. He immediately instructed the sales representative to remove the billboard from the property by Monday of the following week.

Ten minutes later the general manager from the billboard company called back and apologized for the rude behavior of his sales representative and wanted to smooth things out. Before the call with the sales representative, my client was willing to settle for between $1,000 and $2,000 in monthly rent and would have been ecstatic if they agreed. Since the incident with the sales representative, he became convinced that he would not budge on rent. Two weeks later, my client ended up reaching an agreement with the billboard company: $4,000 monthly starting rent with $500 escalators every couple of years. More importantly, adding $4,000 per month in revenue and NOI, my client increased his property value by at least $960,000, simply because billboards are perceived as a very low-risk investment in the marketplace and are often valued at 3.5-5.00% CAP rates. A $4,000 per month or $48,000 per year increase in NOI at 5.00% CAP equates to a $960,000 increase in valuation.

Added Monthly Revenue from Billboard Lease	$4,000
Annual NOI & Cash Flow Boost	**$48,000**
Market CAP Rate for Asset Type	4.85%
Instant Equity Gain	**$989,690**

I saw my client a few weeks ago, and he mentioned that the billboard company had reached out to him, offering north of $500,000 if they can just buy a perpetual easement to use the billboard instead of paying monthly rent. So much for assigning $0 value to billboard income at the time of a $1,700,000 purchase of land by both buyer and seller! Anyway, I walked my client through the calculation above and advised him not to consider anything less than $1,000,000 if he needed the money. But if he does not need the money, I advised him to hang on to it as long as he can, because it will only increase in value. Five years from now, it will perhaps be worth $1.5M-$2M.

In this example, it was a rather expensive property to buy at a $1,700,000 original cost. There are a lot of smaller properties with billboards on them that have minimum rent from the billboard that can be bought for $500,000-$1,000,000 for the value of the building or land itself. In such instances, there is an opportunity to buy a property for its market value, renegotiate the billboard lease, or wait until whatever lease that is in place expires, sell the billboard or perpetual easement for the billboard for what you paid for the entire property or more, and end up with the property you originally purchased for free.

Not all streets and not all billboards are the same. The rent you can earn for a billboard is a factor of how many vehicles drive by it each day. That is how billboards come up with pricing when they quote prospective advertisers how much it will cost them to rent one. So the easiest way to determine what you can actually get on a billboard lease is to simply call the billboard company and ask how much they will charge you to rent an ad at that particular billboard. Most billboards are double-sided, so simply take 40-50% of the total revenue that billboard company makes off a particular billboard, and you can use it as your basis for how much rent you can reasonably ask the billboard company to pay you.

6

RAW LAND

"Raw land often has more hidden income sources than most
improved properties do."

RURAL LAND—TIMBERING

Another great way to acquire real estate for free, or close to
it, is through timbering. Larger tracts of land in rural areas,
such as hunting land, mountain land, farms, or just natural
forest land, can oftentimes be bought for under $500 per acre.
Since little to no development activity may be going on in a
rural area two hours outside the nearest metropolitan area, it's
hard for real estate entrepreneurs to envision how they can
make money on such land. We are accustomed to assuming
that the only way to make money on land is through rezoning
or entitlements to create value, or if you can buy land that is
in a "path of growth," so you can benefit from accelerated or
forced appreciation. However, there are many ways that you

can make a lot of money on rural land that is "in the middle of nowhere." The simplest of such ways is timber management.

Mature timber can range from $800 to $2,000 per acre and sometimes as high as $5,000 per acre depending on timber age, size, type, and quality. A simple way to create cash flow off otherwise non-income producing raw land is timbering. You can buy land in a rural area for $500-$1,000 per acre, sell mature timber off that property for the same amount or more that you paid for the entire tract of land, and therefore get such track of land for free.

We have established that timber is a valuable commodity. On average, most landowners only have timber harvested on a large scale once or twice during ownership. In this case, it is important to think ahead and implement a few simple plans before you sell your timber so that you can achieve the optimum return on the sale.

It is important to begin by verifying your property lines, preferably with your existing survey or by making the small investment of purchasing a current boundary survey. Marking groups of trees with spray-painted marks at boundary corners will ensure the timbering operations remain within the bounds of your land. Once you've established your boundaries, take the important step of discussing your plan with a service forester who can help you create a timbering plan. Service foresters do not participate in timber sales, but many can offer you information about timber buyers and harvesters. They can also advise you on what to expect with timbering contracts and processes such as clear cutting vs. selective harvesting, stumping, etc. You should also obtain multiple bids to ensure you are selling at full market value. Your bid should include the "stumpage price," or the price for trees still standing on their stumps. Variables that are considered when pricing timber include species, size, straightness of trees, distance to their lumber mill, demand, and other factors.

It is hard to carry non-income producing properties long term due to carrying costs. However, if you recouped your investment through timbering the land you just bought, and with your cost basis in land now being $0, it becomes much easier to hold on to it for future appreciation or for personal recreational use, such as hunting. Then you can take your recouped investment and go to the next tract of land and do the same thing.

The most common way people get properties for free is through inheritance. Unfortunately for me, I have no rich uncles to leave "free" properties for me to inherit. That is why I like to create my own "luck" and especially like the deals where I can structure acquisition in a way for me to get some properties free of cost. Real estate is the most powerful wealth creation tool, and if used correctly, it has the same effect as you creating and controlling your own "lottery" or "inheritance." You also have the option to do it as often as you mentally can handle!

Even if you do not have cash funds to make your initial land purchase, since raw land far away from a city is hard to sell and usually sits on the market for a long time, you can structure your acquisition very creatively with owner financing. Sellers of rural land are much more open to selling land on owner financing with deferred payments and deferred interest accrual than sellers of infill urban real estate that is high in demand.

I have purchased land before with as little as a $1,000 down payment with the first payment not due for 90-180 days. If you have a good timber broker that knows what he is doing, 90 days should be plenty of time for you to have timber surveyed, priced individually or in bulk, perform a comprehensive marketing campaign, and hold an auction to sell off the timber—all before your first interest payment is due. So you can literally accumulate hundreds and even thousands of acres of raw land with little to no money out of pocket.

While this is a great strategy to accumulate large amounts of acreage with little to no money out of pocket, I would always recommend reinvesting a portion of your gains from timbering back into reseeding quality timber, so you can secure cash flow for yourself from the property again in the future.

Reseeding timber should run you approximately $80-$100 per acre, as of the date of this publication.

Purchase of Large Land Tract (300ac @ $1,000/ac)	-$300,000
Sell off Mature Timber ($1200/ac avg)	+$360,000
Marketing & Sale Cost ($100/ac)	-$30,000
Re-seeding Cost ($100/ac)	-$30,000
Net Acquisition Cost of Land After 90 days	**$0.00**

Once your land has been timbered and you have recouped your acquisition cost of the land, you can still use inexpensive ways to create more ongoing cash flow off your land without having to wait 14-25 years for the next set of mature timber to grow. You can utilize some of the same strategies to generate income and cash flow off timbered land that we have discussed earlier for urban properties:

- If your land is along a highway, you can possibly install billboards or lease land to have one or more installed by a billboard company.

- You may be able to use the extra space in urban and suburban areas for cell tower and antenna use. You probably will not realize the same rental rates as you will get from a rooftop in a highly populated urban area, but even if limited, extra rental income is extra income that can help pay property taxes on the land. As my business partner Vincenzo likes to say, it's "Pennies from Heaven."

If you look at a map of the United States, what you will see is an occasional grey area or section—these are your metropolitan areas and developed cities. However, 80% of what you are going to see on the map will be green. These green areas (80% if not 90% of US territories) are rural, undeveloped land tracts. So the potential market for this opportunity is really endless. I would estimate that there are four to five times more opportunities in rural areas than you will find in a developed area. Yet, competition in rural areas for these opportunities is virtually nonexistent. If my passion was to just make money and not to develop urban infill mixed-use properties, I would be buying raw rural land all day long.

RURAL LAND—MINING RIGHTS

If you have a large enough tract of land, it is likely that such land will have one or more types of natural resources below the surface. With some simple soil borings and engineering studies, you can determine if your land has mineral resources that can be mined, such as coal (thermal coal as well as metallurgical coal), natural gas, oil, sand, and other natural resources.

However, building the infrastructure and setting up a mining operation, even for the simplest types of natural resources, such as sand, is very expensive and will cost millions, if not tens of millions, of dollars. Also, if you are not experienced in mining, you may lose your investment even if you have $100 million to invest in infrastructure. It is a full-time specialty business to run a mining operation.

If you identify mineral resources on your property, I recommend simply leasing your mineral rights to a major player, preferably a billion dollar or publicly traded company, who does it professionally and has resources to manage expensive change orders that surely will occur when running a mining operation.

Since most of my investment experience has been limited to the East Coast of the United States, I am not familiar with oil or gas operations, as those are more common in states such as Texas or Alaska. But I am familiar with coal operations, as I had invested as a passive investor with friends who owned and operated coal mines. So, I will use metallurgical "met" coal for example purposes in this chapter.

As of the date of this publication, medium-grade met coal was trading around $118-$120 per metric ton. Extraction costs per ton can vary depending on whether or not the mine is operated by union or independent miners and whether or not the miner owns the equipment or is leasing it. How far the mine is located from the nearest wash plant, whether or not certain logistics infrastructure (such as railroads) is in place nearby, and many other important factors will dictate your ultimate extraction cost.

The coal mines that I was involved in averaged $60-$65 per metric ton for extraction cost, which is typical for an average-size mine. With that said, all of these factors should not be of concern to you if you act as just a landowner with coal reserves underneath that you are looking to lease on a mineral-rights lease.

So, as a landowner you can reasonably expect $1.50-$2.00 per ton royalty as a lease rate on every ton of coal mined out of your land. When executing a mineral lease on your property that is structured on a "per ton" basis, I recommend including some performance minimums in the lease. For example, your mineral lease can state that the lease payment shall be $2.00 per every ton of low-vol metallurgical coal mined, with a minimum of 100,000 tons per year.

If the market price of coal drops due to the political climate or other reasons, and the company that leases your land stops the operation for a period of time, they still will be obligated to pay you a certain annual minimum to maintain the lease rights. It is likely that a mining company will not walk away from their multi-million-dollar investment in infrastructure and would prefer to maintain its lease by paying for a minimum performance volume.

It is hard to secure a mineral-rights lease, but if you do, consider it as if you just won a lottery because it can create significant cash flow and equity for you from an otherwise non-income-producing tract of raw land.

Royalty per Metric Ton of Coal Mines	$2.00
Annual Performance Minimum (tons/year)	100,000
Minimum Annual NOI & Cash Flow Boost	**$200,000**
Market CAP Rate for Asset Type	10.00%
Instant Equity Gain	**$2,000,000**

While equity gain may not be that significant and is probably less than the value of the raw land by itself, keep in mind that this example is based on an annual performance minimum of 100,000 tons per year. An average small mine should produce about 50,000-70,000 tons *per month* under normal market conditions.

In the case of mineral-rights leases, monthly or annual cash flow is more important than the value of that future cash flow on a re-investment market (capitalization rate). A $2.00 per ton royalty on a 50,000 ton per month production will yield you a monthly cash flow of $100,000. Such monthly cash flow will likely be enough for most investors to be able to never work another day in their lives and maintain a comfortable lifestyle.

RURAL LAND—OTHER OPTIONS

There are many other ways to make money on raw land besides timbering, mineral-rights leases, and other options I have discussed earlier. These include leasing hunting rights, farming rights, or conservation easements. I encourage you to research other options!

The opportunities to make money on rural raw land are just as abundant as on infill, highly developed, urban properties. They are probably even more abundant, as there are likely fewer use restrictions on raw land in the middle of nowhere than on an inner-city property.

Investing in rural, raw land can be very lucrative, but as with all aspects of life or business, it requires a full-time effort and deliberate focus in order to achieve extraordinary results in this arena. So, you have to decide for yourself where

your passion lies—infill development or countryside—and
pick your sector of real estate specialization based on those
preferences.

Sometimes you do not know what you like more until
you try everything, so I would encourage you to venture into
diverse sectors of real estate (if time and resources permit) so
you can arrive at this conclusion based on your own personal
experience. Over the course of my career, I have certainly
experimented with a lot of property types and projects before
I identified the ones that move my passion gauges.

URBAN LAND—SHORT PLATTING

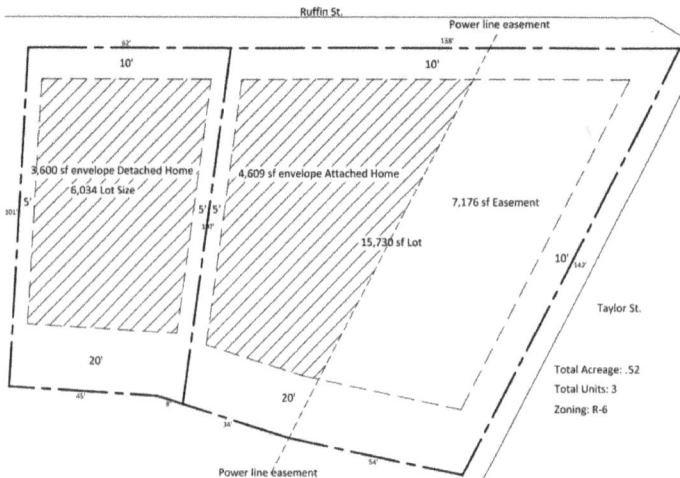

Investment strategies around raw land are not limited
to rural areas with highly motivated sellers. There are also
many opportunities to acquire properties for free in urban,

highly competitive, and developed markets. You just need to be educated enough on your area to be able to recognize those opportunities quickly. Let me give you few examples.

Back in the early days when I used to do all kinds of urban infill projects, including residential construction, I would frequently come across residential houses sitting on double lots. I recognized early on that this was a potential gold mine and would identify every "ghost" lot in infill areas of my city. I would proactively reach out to those owners to see if I could buy their property for the value of the house. While some owners may give or demand extra consideration for having a larger lot, this aspect of the property usually gets overlooked by sellers and buyers. The parties usually treat it as an intangible "bonus" to the transaction.

Here is an example of one such house I purchased for the value of the house at $370,000. I thought it was a fair price for the house given the condition it was in. I thought that if I spent $50,000 on renovating the house, I could probably sell it for $525,000-$575,000 on the open market.

After getting it under contract and reading the legal description, I realized that the legal description calls for this property to be two lots, while the GIS map and the county website showed the property as one lot. This is a common scenario with the second lot known as a "ghost" lot. But since the property only has one tax ID and one tax bill, many sellers are not even aware that their house sits on two lots that do not need to be subdivided.

So even though the property is showing on the city GIS as a single parcel, with a single tax ID number, I can very easily subdivide it into two lots, and I can do so without even going through a formal subdivision process. The only thing I need to do in order to "subdivide" this property is to order a survey to trace and reinstate "ghost" lot lines and then call the city and ask them to update their GIS map according to the original plat from when this subdivision was originally platted and recorded. This process should take no longer than a few days, and in the end you should have two subdivided parcels with two tax ID numbers.

So in this case, my deal went from solid base hit to a home run. I bought the house for $370,000. After doing $50,000 of renovations, I sold the house for $580,000, making a profit of $130,000 after selling costs. But more importantly, I called the county and asked them to update the map to show this property as two lots instead of one. Less than 24 hours later, the map was updated showing two lots, with the second lot having an assessed value of $180,000. So even if I were to sell the house the next day for the same price that I paid for it, I would have made a pure profit of $180,000 by keeping the second lot free and clear.

Purchase Price of Infill House	-$370,000
Short-Platting Cost	-$0
Sale Price of the House	+$370,000
Value of Remaining Short Platted SF Lot	**$180,000**

In this particular case, I did not sell the extra lot like I have done many times before, and instead I built another house on that lot and sold the new construction house, making an extra profit of $150,000 in addition to the built-in profit I had in the land. The important thing to note here is that having the extra lot free and clear enabled me to get construction financing to finance 100% of the cost of a new construction house since I was able to demonstrate $180,000 of perceived equity in the deal, which met the down payment requirements for the bank.

In the end, the profits from the extra little lot totaled over $330,000, which is almost 3x more than the profit I was going to make just on the house had I not recognized the "ghost lot" opportunity that was hiding in plain sight of the seller and other investors who looked at the house.

Again, even in highly competitive infill markets, there are still plenty of ways to acquire high-demand properties for free if you truly understand the area and the rules of the real estate game. Deals where I can get properties for free are my favorite types of deals. Getting real estate for free has become a personal passion and a hobby of mine.

I have purchased many houses like this around my city that came with large lots, which I was able to subdivide. After selling the house for about the same price that I paid for it, I ended up with one or two (or more) lots worth $100,000-$250,000 each for free that I can then sell separately or build on.

When I was a kid in my early twenties, I used to do a bunch of single-family flips. A typical flip for me back then would usually mean a remodel of an older property to create equity. It takes time and requires additional investment beyond the purchase price. A lot of things can go wrong during construction, such as change orders from contractors.

If I had to do it all over again, I would only be doing short-platting of houses on large lots. As demonstrated in the example above, short-platting is a much cleaner way to "flip" single-family homes for significant profit without doing any actual remodeling work, even if you sold the property for exactly the same price that you purchased it for.

If the urban lot that you ended up with free of cost is commercially zoned, you can also rent it for parking instead of selling. If you plan to not sell it right away, you still have to pay property taxes to be able to carry it long-term. It is always good to have a way for the property to pay for its own carrying costs so that it does not become a cash flow burden for you—known as an alligator.

Simply described, alligators are properties that have negative cash flow. All alligators behave the same way and have one common goal in mind—to drag you underwater and keep you there. If the alligator is big enough or keeps you underwater long enough, sooner or later you are almost guaranteed to drown financially. Negative cash flow is a finite number. Always get rid of alligators in your life at your earliest opportunity.

If your lot is located in a residential area, its zoning does not permit the renting of parking, and there are no other ways to create cash flow off the lot, then I recommend selling the property right away or developing an income-producing structure on it due to the reasons described above. You do not want to have any real property that has no cash flow and requires regular cash infusions out of pocket to maintain it. These expenses could include the cutting of grass, maintaining security, and paying property taxes.

URBAN LAND—REZONING

Rezoning properties to accommodate their highest development potential is probably the oldest and most common investment strategy relative to raw land. The basic concept of rezoning described in layman terms is very simple—an acre of raw land zoned as residential in your city may be valued at $100,000 per acre. Yet the same acre of land rezoned to commercial use may trade at $1,000,000 per acre. Rezoning is a very powerful tool since it requires no physical change to the land, other than changing its zoning designation on paper to accommodate more intense uses.

The rezoning process in most municipalities requires a multi-step public hearing. Steps include notifying your neighbors and adjoining property owners of your plans to rezone a property, holding public neighborhood and city advisory council "CAC" hearings, planning board hearings and a review process, and of course City Council hearings. It is the City Council who will ultimately vote on your zoning case based on feedback from the neighbors and recommendations from the planning board of your municipality.

With so many people involved in the process who have different opinions, a lot of things can potentially go against you along the way. Successful rezoning is never guaranteed. It usually requires attorney representation, political maneuvering, and negotiations with the community leaders. Most, if not all, rezoning cases that I have successfully completed were "conditional use" cases, meaning that I had to offer certain conditions to appease the neighbors and the city council members in order to achieve my desired zoning for a particular property.

Zoning conditions that I had to offer in the past were often very practical in nature—such as agreeing to limit density beyond what zoning allows and increase the parking ratios above what is permitted by code. But zoning conditions can also be more subjective in nature—such as agreeing to build public art to enhance the community, agreeing to impose limits on building materials out of which a future project will be constructed to ensure they are high quality, and agreeing to limit the number of bedrooms and bathrooms in future units to be constructed to discourage certain types of residents from leasing or purchasing units in the future development (such as students who typically reside in a 4BD/4BA units near universities).

When you buy a property, the zoning guidelines that come with it come to you by a right that no one can take away. So, when going through a rezoning process, it is the neighbors' opportunity to have a say into what can be built next door to them. That is why most zoning cases I have been involved in were very political in nature. Yet, once you have done a few and get a good handle on the process of rezoning, rezoning opportunities can prove to be very lucrative, as you will see from a few examples below.

EXAMPLES OF RECENT REZONINGS

Imagine a 10,000 sqft single story building sitting on 0.5 acres of land in the downtown area of your city. It's an old industrial building that has been converted to entertainment use and has been used as a nightclub for the past 40 years. Although the building is single story, everything around the property has been rezoned and redeveloped into high rise buildings as the area grew and developed.

The property was owned and operated by an owner-user; that's why this building was never rezoned or redeveloped like the rest of the neighborhood. As many entertainment and hospitality venues suffered significant losses amidst the shutdowns of Covid-19, the owners of this particular venue approached us to sell the property with a short-term (two-year) sale leaseback.

It was a creative deal structure with a high price and unattractive leaseback terms, which is why they could not just sell it to anyone on the open market and needed a creative buyer, like myself, to be able to handcraft transaction terms that would get them what they needed on a short closing timeline but where the deal still made sense for me as a buyer. A sale would have given them much-needed liquidity and a cash infusion, while leaseback would give them time to find an alternative location to relocate to. From our perspective, we saw an opportunity to entitle and rezone the site for its highest and best use while having a three-year runway to effectuate our plan with a tenant in place in the meantime.

We purchased the site for what seemed like an astronomical amount of money at the time—$4,000,000 for a single-story 10,000 sqft building on a 0.5 acre lot. Its fair market value was probably closer to $2,500,000 at the time, but we saw this as a unique opportunity to acquire a rare and highly desirable site. We knew that there was the potential to rezone this site for a high-rise tower that could accommodate as many as 300 units, which is exactly what we did.

The rezoning process took us around 90 days to complete; it was probably one of the fastest rezoning processes I have ever done. We rezoned the site to DX-40, which allowed for a 40-story building. Almost immediately after the completion of rezoning, we contracted to sell the site for the going rate of DX-40 land—which at the time was $370/sqft or $8,100,000. That price was double the "high" price we paid just a few months prior. The new buyer, a large national developer, has subsequently entitled the site to develop a 385-unit, 32-story tower on the subject property.

Purchase Price of the Site	$4,000,000
Pursuit & Rezoning Costs	$40,000
Value before Rezoning	$2,500,000
Value after Rezoning: $40,000/door	$8,100,000
Equity Gain from a Successful Rezoning	**$4,060,000**

As you can see from the example above, rezoning is a very, very powerful tool. Outside of top prizes on a few major lotteries, most lottery jackpots do not yield even close to four million dollars in gains. The beauty of this business is that it gives you an opportunity to create and control your own lottery wins as often as you want, depending on how hard you want to work and how well you learn the business. To be able to recognize and capitalize on these opportunities that are all around us, you just need to have a fluent, up-to-date knowledge of your marketplace comps and an intimate under-standing of your local unified development ordinance (UDO) and zoning codes.

Real estate is a big-money sport, and if you want to take this sport of real estate investing seriously, I would recommend studying your local municipality's UDO cover to cover and staying up to date on upcoming changes to the ordinance. Know the code better than your engineers, attorneys, and architects do. Remember that small changes in demand for real estate create big results, and a small text change to one section of your city's development ordinance can potentially mean millions of dollars of profit to you if you get up to speed on it before the masses do.

MORE REZONING

I cannot stress enough how important and powerful the tool of rezoning is. I want to instill the potential of this tool into your brain. So let me give you another example of a rezoning case that we completed a few years ago in the heart of the downtown in my city.

The site is located a half mile from the campus of North Carolina State University and is virtually across the street from another institution, Meredith College. It is also located on one of the main arteries into downtown Raleigh—Hillsbor-ough Street. This particular street has been neglected over the past few decades, with many dilapidated one- and two-story buildings. However, over the past ten years, the street has undergone major transformations and redevelopment, both from the private sector and from the public sector, such as renovating the streetscape, redoing the sidewalks, landscaping, etc. Whenever there is significant investor attention to a certain part of town with hundreds of millions of dollars being invested into redevelopment of the area—read that as an opportunity for you to get involved right in the middle of the action.

In this scenario, imagine a boarded-up, former convenience store/gasoline station building most recently used as a tobacco shop, an empty lot overgrown with weeds, and a dozen old, single-family homes and duplexes in various stages of disrepair—all owned by various owners who have had these properties for decades. Aesthetically unattractive, these properties seemed destined to remain dormant as the surrounding area rapidly redeveloped into mixed use retail/multi-family and student-housing properties. Among those weeds and blight, we saw a vision for this property. We wanted to redevelop it into something new and beautiful to be consistent with what was happening on the street, including some of our own projects we acquired or developed a few years prior.

We approached all of the landowners, which was not easy since most had owned their properties in their families for 20-50 years, and secured contracts to purchase their properties with assurances of cooperation and ample time before closing. The negotiation and assemblage process took approximately 48 months for all thirteen parcels on this site. But once secured under option agreements, we got to work on rezoning, which took another 18 months.

The properties were zoned Neighborhood Mixed Use (three stories) or NX-3. During our review of the UDO, we determined that the future land use plan for the subject site called for rezoning it to NX-7, allowing for mixed use up to seven stories. In this case, a set of old homes, an empty lot, and a deteriorating, boarded-up tobacco shop, when rezoned to their highest and best use, could accommodate two large, seven-story buildings on 3.5 acres of land, totaling 450 units.

GARAGE ENTRY / FIRE PUMP / TRASH

BUILDING 1

BUILDING 2

BUILDING 1

BUILDING 2
ALTERNATE LAYOUT - 31 UNITS / LEVEL

GARAGE ENTRY / FIRE PUMP / TRASH

Due to the proximity to universities, the site can be developed either into a student-housing product or market-rate apartments.

The purpose of this example is to demonstrate how a simple rezoning process creates significant equity and profit without doing anything physical to the property itself. When we contracted the thirteen parcels of land subject to this site, they were limited to the number of units that you can fit within a three-story building on 3.5 acres of land. At the time we started this assemblage, the going rate per square of land of a three-story zoned property on this street was approximately $40/sqft of land or $30,000 per door on a multifamily play. So a

3.5 acre tract in this location would trade at approximately $6 million dollars (3.5 acres x 43,560 sqft per acre x $40 per sqft = $6,098,400 million), which is approximately what we had paid for the land—a little under six million dollars. By the time we finished assembling and rezoning the site, the going rate for multifamily land had appreciated to be around $40,000 per door. Having successful completed rezoning of the property for higher density, we were now able to put 450 units on the site, thus increasing the property's value to approximately $18,000,000 (450 units x $40,000 per unit = $18,000,000).

Purchase Price of the Site	$6,000,000
Pursuit & Rezoning Costs	$200,000
Total Cost of Acquisition	$6,200,000
Value before Rezoning: $30,000/door	$6,000,000
Value after Rezoning: $40,000/door	$18,000,000
Equity Gain from a Successful Rezoning	**$11,800,000**

If we chose to sell this site today, we should be able to get $18,000,000 for it on the open market and realize a ~$12,000,000 gain. Not a bad return on a $200,000 investment into rezoning on optioned land. Right now, however, is not the best time to sell multifamily land as the lending climate has tightened for new-construction multifamily. So we think that if we hold on to the site and time the market, we can really maximize the value and possibly achieve as high as $50,000 per door or higher in a few years. Timing the market is just as important in this business as everything else.

URBAN LAND—ENTITLEMENTS

Whenever rezoning is not possible, there are other ways to create significant value on urban land tracts that do not require any physical improvements to be done on the land. The simplest way to create equity in land out of "thin air" is through the entitlement process.

Raw land, even if it's well-located in the city limits, is just a raw piece of land with no income and speculative theories of what can be built on it. Even if such theories are based on existing zoning designations that govern what can be built on it, without an engineered and approved set of plans (i.e. "entitlements"), nothing is guaranteed and there is a certain level of risk associated with buying a raw piece of dirt that is not entitled for a specific project. Therefore, it is a very logical conclusion that builders and developers are willing to pay more for raw land and close faster if the land comes with certain entitlements for a specific project. Taking raw land through an entitlement process eliminates entitlement risk and time for developers. That in-turn creates a premium on what they are willing to pay for a ready-to-go, fully-engineered and development project.

I have found that the cost of engineering a project on a raw piece of land usually yields 300%-5,000% profit margin on your investment into entitlement costs, depending on the size, the nature, and the location of the project. Let me demonstrate how this concept works on one example that I completed in my city.

I contracted to buy an old daycare facility sitting on 3.76 acres of land for what it was worth as an old daycare—$675,000.

The property backed up to a local community park on one side and on the other side to one of the most prestigious golf communities in the area. This is a high-demand area, yet it had a very limited supply of new housing construction. The property was zoned R-4, meaning a low-density residential zoning with a maximum of four dwelling units per acre. My first thought was to take it through the rezoning process to increase density from four units per acre (R-4) to at least 10 units per acre (R-10). However, after the first neighborhood meeting, I quickly realized that this rezoning case would be an uphill battle, as neighbors with houses to the north really liked their large open backyard and did not want to see anything developed here.

So I withdrew our rezoning case after the first hearing and looked into the possibility of what could be done with the property the way it sits under current zoning. The daycare use was not compliant, but it was grandfathered in and could continue to operate as a daycare. But other than that, no commercial use was permitted on the property.

We engaged an engineer to come up with an actual lot yield of how many houses we could fit on the site after factoring in the setbacks, new road construction, stormwater management, and other fun limitation factors of the development world. Although zoning allowed up to 15 single family homes (3.76 acres x 4 units per acre = 15 houses), the engineer was only able to come up with a maximum lot yield of 11 lots.

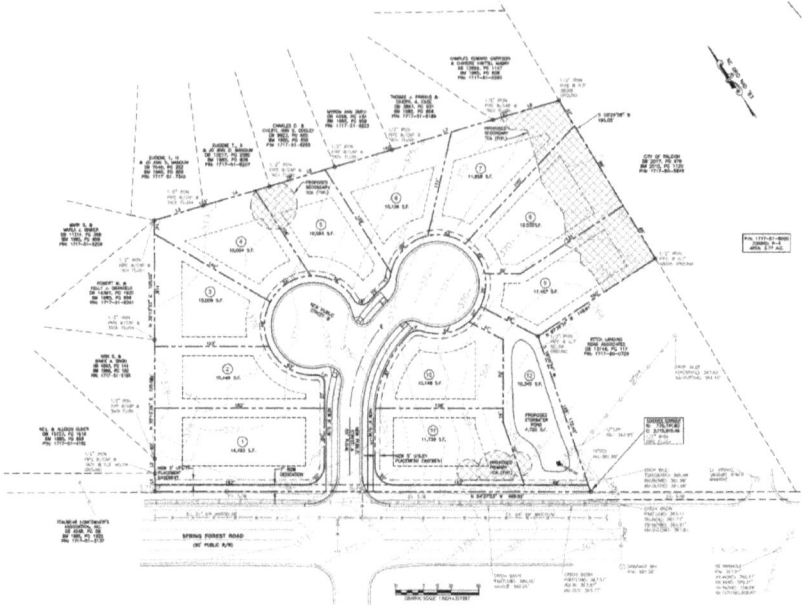

11 single family lots on 3.76 acres seemed like a gross underutilization of property. However, intimate knowledge of the market rates resulted in a quick realization that the going price for single-family lots in this high-demand area was about $225,000 per developed lot. It does not take a math genius to figure out that the market value of these 11 lots will be approximately $2.5 million dollars upon completion. $675,000 for land acquisition, $75,000 for engineering and permits, and another $450,000 to develop a small cul-de-sac and lot infrastructure would have an all-in cost of $1.2 million. So even with this low unit yield, the project made sense with the potential to double the money on the land.

Also, if we decide to build the houses, there would potentially be another $2-$2.5 million profit on the construction of 11 homes. We engaged the engineer to take the property through the entitlement process during our contract period. With highly vocal neighbors all around us, I did not want to close on the land until I knew that my development plans would be approved by the city, so I negotiated extensions on the contract to allow time for entitlements, which took about nine months to complete.

Halfway through the entitlement process, I was approached by a local builder who wanted to take the project off my hands for a discounted price. Under this scenario I just needed to finish the paperwork process for permitting and would not have to physically develop the property. The builder would then make some money on land development to reduce his entry point per lot to mitigate the risk on house construction. This is exactly what I did—contracted to sell the property subject to my finishing the permitting and construction drawings for this small subdivision for $1.35 million or about double the amount of the original option price. Once we received the permits, we closed on the purchase at $675,000 two weeks later. We closed on the sale at $1,350,000 the very next day.

Purchase Price at Fair Market Value as a Daycare	$675,000
Cost of Entitlement	$75,000
Value of Developed Lots Less Development Cost	$2,000,000
Discounted Price of Entitled Land on a Quick Flip	$1,350,000
Total Cost	$750,000
Total Out of Pocket Cost	$75,000
Sale Price	$1,350,000
Profit Gain from 1 day of ownership	**$600,000**

In this case, investment into the entitlement process of $75,000 yielded a 1,600%+ gain in equity (a $1.25 million equity gain on a $75,000 investment into engineering), but we settled for a 50% discount of 800% gain in exchange for a quick close without a need to perform any of the actual physical development activity on the property ($600,000 profit from 1 day of ownership on a $75,000 investment into engineering).

Rezoning and entitlement are both powerful tools to create significant equities out of "thin air" without doing anything physical to the property such as expensive site development work, but they require your up-to-date knowledge of the marketplace as well as of your local zoning and development codes. In my company, 50% of team resources and time are being spent on identifying opportunities to rezone or entitle under-utilized properties in prime locations. On any given day of the week we have at least 10-12 such projects going at the same time, aside from our long-term developments. Those that we do not care about, are "fillers" and candidates for a "flip" to generate cash in order to be able to develop, see through to the end, and then keep those deals that we care about.

The ones that we care about are usually determined by a single criteria, which is very simple—location. It must be in an absolute prime, signature, romantic location that everyone wants to be in. But to be able to keep projects in prime locations, you need those fillers and flips to generate the fuel necessary to keep the engine of your real estate entrepreneurship going.

Ok, enough about raw land. Let's get back to income-pro-ducing properties and how small changes in operations can make you big bucks

7

UTILITIES

"There is as much profit in
your building expenses as in
your building income."

SUB-METERING UTILITIES

A significant portion of investment-property expenses are attributable to the cost of utilities. Sub-metering utilities is a great way of turning an uncontrollable line item expense into an income source. Investment properties with utility services provided to tenants through a master meter could be a candidate for sub-metering. Electricity, gas, water, and even heating and cooling can be sub-metered.

Sub-metering is typically accomplished by engaging a third-party, turn-key provider that is familiar with the processes and regulations in this arena. The utility sub-metering company will sell, install, read, and service individual meters and provide billing and management services to the property owner. Utilities are billed to tenants who pay the provider, and then reimbursement is made to the property owner. Depending on your provider, equipment and installation costs can either be paid upfront or financed through a variety of plans, such as simple installments, shared revenue, and other methods of extended repayment options.

Here is a simple example of how it works. I bought this 24-unit apartment building near downtown Raleigh back in my early 20s.

It was a historic building built in 1925, and the heat for the units was provided by a central boiler system in the basement that was gas powered. The monthly gas bill that I was paying to power the boiler was approximately $2,100 per month! While doing other renovations to the building right after purchase, a decision was made to get rid of the central boiler system along with the window AC units. They were replaced with individual HVAC units located on the roof in order to pass the cost of heating and cooling to the tenants, like most newer apartments do.

The cost of engineering a split system and installing 24 individual HVAC units was approximately $150,000, but it enabled me to save approximately $2,100 per month on the previous natural gas bill, thus improving the NOI by $25,200 per year. Even though it would take six years to pay back the investment in the event of a long-term hold, $25,200 annual increase in NOI resulted in an instant equity gain of $420,000 at a 6.00% market CAP rate for such an asset type.

Cost of Replacing Boiler with individual HVACs	$150,000
Annual NOI & Cash Flow Boost	$25,200
Market CAP Rate for Asset Type	6.00%
Instant Equity Gain	**$420,000**
Net Gain	$270,000
Instant Return on Investment	280%

Whether your plan is to sell the property after repositioning the NOI or to keep the building long term, the investment makes sense, as you can see in the calculation above.

RATIO UTILITY BILLING SYSTEM

If sub-metering is not an option due to a lack of available space or existing construction obstacles, establishing a Ratio Utility Billing System (RUBS) could be a favorable alternative.

A RUBS is a utility billing method that allocates 100% of your property's utility bill to the tenants based on an occupant factor, square footage, or a combination of both, less a predetermined percentage (determined by the property owner) of common area allowance. The allocation begins with an analysis of the property's utility bills and determines the dollar amount billed for a given consumption period. The predetermined common area allowance percentage is deducted to determine the final amount to be allocated. That amount is then divided by the total units' occupant factor and then multiplied by the individual unit's occupant factor.

Different variables may be used for different utilities and are typically determined by state and local regulations. RUBS requires no initial capital investment and could be implemented for nearly all utilities including water, wastewater, gas, electric and even trash services. Since RUBS is calculated based on the monthly utility bill, a greater percentage of your monthly utility expenses can actually be recovered to optimize your NOI.

Significant state and local regulations govern metering, the sub-metering of utilities, and the implementation of RUBS. Knowledge of your local rules is vital for the success of such an endeavor in order to avoid getting tagged for the unlicensed practice of "providing utility services to consumers."

SOLAR PANELS AND THERMAL BARRIERS

Utility expenses, especially electricity costs, are a significant line item in any investment property budget. Furthermore, it is challenging to curtail these expenses that, for the most part, are generated by tenants based on usage that is difficult to forecast or track on an individual basis. In many areas of the United States and abroad, solar energy is a viable alternative. By making an upfront investment in equipment, partially offset by first-year federal tax credits, a property owner could realize a remarkable reduction in utility expenses. Solar energy systems are passive operating systems, seamlessly integrating with existing utilities. Since 2010, the average cost of solar PV panels has dropped more than 60% and the cost of a solar electric system has dropped by 50%.

Passive operation, seamless integration with existing power sources, and very low maintenance are all reasons why solar systems are welcomed by local jurisdictions. Installation costs have become more cost effective in recent years, and local utility providers have also eased energy buy-back restrictions. Once you determine the power level in kilowatts used in your building and coordinate with a solar provider to establish panel requirements, the calculation of energy buy back becomes quite simple.

As a property owner, harnessing your operating expenses is one of the most important steps you can take on the path to greater profitability. This section addresses the benefits associated with harnessing the power of the sun and how it can play a role in drastically reducing utility expenses and optimizing your NOI.

As discussed in the Cell Tower section, your building's rooftop is an opportunity to generate income. In the case of solar energy, rooftop solar would be evaluated based on a calculated return on investment or ROI in the form of significant reductions in utility expenses. As of the time of publishing, a one-time, 30% federal tax credit is offered to those who install solar energy systems, typically assigned to the company installing your system and serving as a reduction in up-front costs.

Solar electricity is generated by a group of solar panels, or an array, installed on the roof of your building. When sunlight falls on the solar panels, electric current is created and fed into an inverter that changes it to the standard electricity your building already uses. The inverter acts as an energy manager, using solar-generated energy first, and then supplementing it with utility power on an as-needed basis. There is even a process called net metering that allows consumers to sell surplus solar energy back to utility companies, which further offsets electric expenses and adds revenue to boost your NOI.

When considering rooftop solar energy, you must do some homework and hire an experienced professional to install and maintain your system. Your first step should be to carefully evaluate the age and integrity of the existing roof. A typical rooftop solar energy system is based on a 25-year lifespan. Therefore, your roof must be capable of sustaining an installation for at least that long, including the ability to handle the weight of the solar energy system. Incompatibility in roof and solar-energy system lifespans could add unanticipated costs. These costs could include paying to remove and reinstall the solar panels during roof repair or replacement or an extended disruption of solar energy during construction.

Your solar energy professional will walk you through the process of analyzing the current and historic electric usage of your building and will decide what size system is needed for the building. Cost proposals typically include installation and maintenance and account for the one-time tax credit (in the US). Most solar companies also offer installment programs that can spread out the installation costs over time, providing for a more manageable outlay of capital.

Most retail and residential properties, such as apartment buildings, already have tenants paying for individual electric bills. However, in situations where there is a common electric meter, such as hotels, senior housing, or office buildings, installing a solar system can be quite beneficial. The following example illustrates what type of savings could be achieved if your average electric bill is $1,500 per month on a small office building that is leased on a full-service basis with the landlord paying common electric bills.

Average Annual Electric Expenses	$18,000
Initial Cost of Solar Panel System	$150,000
One-Time 30% Federal Tax Credit	$45,000
Total Out of Pocket Cost	$105,000
Annual NOI Gain from Electric Savings	**$18,000**
Market CAP Rate for Asset Type	8.50%
Instant Equity Gain	**$211,764**
Net Equity Gain from Solar System Installation	**+$106,764**

Most solar companies offer in-house financing options with as little as a $0 down payment. You can realize the benefit of solar energy without any upfront cash outlay, where your payment can be equal to or less than what your monthly electric bill is. The following are some finance options that I have been offered by various solar companies in the past on a $40,000 solar system installation:

20 Year Term Loan @ 5.99%	$286/mo
10 Year Term Loan @ 4.99%	$424/mo
18 months Cash @ 0%	$2,224/mo

There are many other things that you can do as a landlord to decrease utility costs and optimize NOI. A simple search on the internet will yield thousands of pages of information that can provide you with different ideas on achieving energy efficiency. For example, installing a thermal barrier in the attic of a residential house rental will result in approximately a 20% cost reduction on the electric bill. If such an exercise costs you

$2,500 to implement but results in a 20% savings on a $300 monthly electric bill, or $60 per month, even in a 10% CAP market on residential rentals, this would result in an instant equity gain of $7,200, or nearly a 300% return on investment.

A friend of mine told me that he knows one real estate investor in the San Francisco area whose entire business model is centered around buying large office buildings, doing nothing to the buildings other than changing how utilities are paid, making them more efficient or otherwise reducing or deferring the utility costs to the tenants, optimizing NOI, and putting the buildings back on the market within 12 months after utility rearrangement is complete with a new, improved NOI for a multi-million-dollar profit.

With countless new technologies available today to optimize energy efficiency, there are innumerable options you can explore to save on utility bills and improve NOI on your investment properties.

8

MASTER LEASES

"Staying educated on rent comps in your area can single-handedly change your life."

MASTER LEASING—AS A CASH FLOW TOOL

The number of powerful tools in a real estate toolbox is practically endless. We have already discussed in this book many tools that are available to you as a real estate entrepreneur, each capable of making significant changes in your investment portfolio cash flow and equity positions. The concept of master leases is yet another such tool that can single-handedly set you on a path of financial freedom.

Let's assume that you are a new investor just starting your career path in the sport of real estate acquisitions. You have not yet accumulated a large portfolio of income-producing buildings generating enough cash flow to pay for your lifestyle.

Yet, you have done your research on market value and sale and lease comparables. You have current market knowledge, and you recognize opportunities in your market. You just do not know where to get the money to capitalize on them and acquire your first building.

You feel like you are stuck and opportunities are passing you by. If only you had the cash to capitalize on them. Do not get discouraged, because there is an excellent tool (among many others) available for people in the same situation as you—master leases. Master leases do not require you to have large amounts of cash to buy an underperforming property. It simply requires your intimate knowledge of rent comps in your area.

I will use residential units for the purposes of this example, although the same concept applies to all real estate assets. There are likely many older apartment complexes in your city that have below-market rents that have not increased over time at the same rate as market demand did. If you study what units are leasing for in your area of focus, you will quickly realize that some properties are leasing for significantly less than other properties in the same general area for no particular reason other than the fact that the owners are not being educated on up-to-date market dynamics in the area. This presents a possibility for you to capitalize on such knowledge without even acquiring the property that you recognize as an opportunity.

Let me give you a personal example of how this works. When I was at the beginning of my real estate career in my late teens, I wanted to buy an 8-unit apartment building in a historic neighborhood near the downtown of my city that was quickly becoming a high-demand area with rising property values and rents.

The building consisted of eight, two-bedroom units that were leasing on average at $550 per unit. Based on my up-to-date knowledge of rent comps, I quickly recognized that the going rate for these types of units at the time was around $795 for a 2BD/1BA unit. The building was not for sale; it just had a "for rent" sign in front. I approached the owners from many different angles about selling the building to me, but they just were not interested in selling.

I was frustrated because I had spent a lot of time on this project. I knew that there was a value-add opportunity here, but it only worked if I had this building in my possession. So I approached the owner one more time and asked him not to sell the building to me but to simply rent to me the one available unit in the building at the going rate of $550 per month as a tenant. The owner obviously agreed, as it was his goal to rent the unit. But then I added a little twist to it—I wanted a right of first refusal to rent the remaining seven units in the building as they became available at the same rate, with the right to sublease the units.

The benefit to the owner was that he had one tenant to worry about, not eight, which guaranteed him 100% occupancy year-round. The building owner liked that idea and agreed to the deal, and we even negotiated a package discounted price of $500 per unit. I rented the entire building with a right to sublease. That is how the concept of master leases first occurred to me at the age of 19. In this case, I was able to sublease units in the building for ~$800 per unit, generating approximately $300 per unit margin, or $2,400 per month of cash flow.

Number of Units in the Building	8 units
Asking Rent per Unit	$500/mo
Marketing Rent per Unit	$800/mo
Cashflow Margin per Unit	$300/mo
Total Monthly Cash Flow Margin	$2,400/mo
Annual Cash Flow Created out of "Thin Air"	**$28,800/year**

At the time, it was a lot of money to me, and I felt like I had just discovered a gold mine. In a sense, it was. The only thing I had to do was to keep the building full and collect rent from the tenants. But other than that, I really did not have to worry about anything else that usually comes with property ownership, such as worrying about maintenance expenses, property taxes, insurance, etc. I did not have to come up with a down payment to buy the property, secure loans, or seek investors. I was just a tenant in a building like many others.

If I got a call from my tenant who said, "Hey, my HVAC is not working." I simply picked up the phone, called the building owner, and said, "Hi, this is your tenant Nikita from unit seven. My HVAC is not working. Can you come fix it?" If I got a call from a different tenant that said his toilet was clogged, I simply picked up the phone, called the building owner, and said, "Hi, this is Nikita, your tenant from unit three; my toilet is clogged."

You get the point; all expenses in the case of a master lease situation are passed through to the building owner.

Since that first building, the concept of master leases has really hit home for me. I discovered a way to get the main benefit of property ownership—cash flow—without actually owning the properties themselves. After that first experience, I went on a witch hunt for apartment buildings and even single-family homes in my area that had below-market asking rents. I have master leased everything from parking lots and single-family homes to rooming houses and large apartment buildings. I have done a lot of smaller properties ranging from four to 20 units because it took some time for me to mentally graduate enough to handle a 200-unit apartment complex. But the bigger the property, the more powerful the master lease becomes.

Just consider, for an instance, what a difference this tool can make in your life if you were able to find just one average-size apartment complex of 276 units in your city in which units are leasing for an average of $800/mo with market rents of $985/mo. Even if you were not able to negotiate a 10% vacancy discount factor on your master lease rate, although most owners would gladly consider that, a nominal $185 per month cash flow margin per unit will yield you a total cash flow of $51,060/mo. For most of the general population in the US, such monthly cash flow usually means financial freedom.

What's great about this concept is that you can literally go out after you finish reading this book and create cash flow for yourself in as little as 30 days if you find the right property. What's even greater is that you do not need the $15-$20 million dollars to buy a 276-unit apartment complex to generate this cash flow. You will maybe need to have enough cash to just put a security deposit down, although you can negotiate that as well since you are not quite a normal tenant.

I can assure you that if you implement the tool of master leases, one day very soon you will find yourself in a position to buy such properties yourself without a need to master lease the units, and then you will realize all the other benefits of property ownership, such as depreciation, appreciation, debt repayment from tenant rents, etc.

I have met people in other states who quickly became my friends and who have master leased everything from large office buildings and self-storage facilities to 600-unit apartment complexes with margins from $50 to $400/mo. Go figure what a $400/mo margin on a 600-unit apartment complex would yield you on a monthly basis. Since then, I have met friends who have built their entire business models around the concept of master leases. What a powerful, powerful tool it is.

Although master leases are not common on apartment buildings, they are pretty widespread on office buildings. There are many companies now, including publicly traded companies, whose entire business model is to lease large blocks of office space and to then convert them to smaller executive office suites to be leased out individually at a higher price per square foot of leasable space.

A company may lease a 10,000-square-foot office suite in an office tower for $30 per square foot and sublease it in smaller increments as individual offices with included utilities and a common conference room, averaging as much as $60 per square foot on leasable space. A lot of companies that adopted this tool as a business model for office space went a step further, offering many add-on services such as phone answering, mail handling, receptionists, etc., for additional revenue. Again, there is endless potential to combine and intermix various real estate tools with each other to multiply revenue and equity.

MASTER LEASING—AS A SALES TOOL

Another way to utilize master leases to maximize your profits is on the sale of the property. Remember that property value is a function of NOI and CAP rate. NOI is the net income that a property generates before debt service, and CAP rate is a perceived measure of risk. If NOI is held constant, and the only thing we could affect is the CAP rate, the tenant mix, their respective lease terms, and their perceived ability to perform on lease obligations all play a role in the perceived level of risk of a particular investment. These factors therefore have a direct effect on what CAP rate the subject property will trade for. This is when a master lease can be a very powerful tool to effectuate CAP rate compression to achieve a higher value and above-market value sales price on your building.

By means of example, I will share a multi-tenant warehouse building I owned in the triad area of North Carolina. It was an old factory built in sections over a couple of decades. Every time the factory wanted to expand, they just built a new addition of 5,000-10,000 sqft to add on to the existing building. As a result, I ended up purchasing this building that was chopped up into 11 distinct 5,000-10,000 sqft sections.

While it was not ideal for a single tenant, I thought such a "chopped up" layout was actually favorable for several smaller users, which presented an opportunity to charge higher rent to smaller users. The issue arose when it came time to sell the building. While the building was mostly leased with few vacant units, the tenants (like most smaller tenants) were not credit tenants and had short-term leases in place, ranging from one to three years in term. Having short-term leases with non-credit, mom-and-pop tenants always results in CAP rate expansion on otherwise totally good, well-located buildings. Again, the CAP rate is a perceived measure of risk, and short-term, non-credit tenants are always perceived as riskier from this perspective.

I paid $1,100,000 for the 54,000-square-foot building, and after spending around $100,000 on renovations, I was able to get it 75% leased with an NOI of $150,000. At full occupancy, NOI would have been $200,000. I wanted to sell the property quickly, but the problem was that the market was only willing to pay me a 10% CAP on existing, or $1,500,000, because of the perceived risk of the tenant mix and their ability to stay and perform long-term. I thought that selling it for $1,500,000 was leaving a lot of money on the table, at least $500,000. I was trying to brainstorm how I could get more money out of this building, and that's when three simultaneous thoughts hit me across the forehead!

First, I can close the vacancy gap and get NOI to $200,000 by leasing the vacant units back myself. The risk would be, if I am unable to sublease the units to actual end-user tenants, then I'd be responsible for paying rent myself. If I were to do a five-year leaseback, then it means I would have to pay

$250,000 in rent over 5 years on space that I'm not using. Although the likelihood that it would have sat vacant for all five years is low. But even in such an event, I would still be better off by $250,000, as I would have achieved a $500,000 higher sales price on the front end. The issue still remains that other tenants have varying lease term durations and are perceived to be non-credit and higher risk in nature.

That's when the second thought came to mind: what if I master leased the whole building before the sale with the right to sublease? People generally pay more (a reduced CAP rate) for a single-tenant building on a longer-term lease. So when I go to sell, I can confidently say that the property is 100% leased to a single tenant on an NNN lease, thus justifying a lower CAP rate. Nevertheless, the CAP rate at which the building will be sold would still be based on the market's opinion about my ability to pay as a single, master tenant of the building.

That's when the third thought occurred to me—what if I completely eliminated the uncertainty factor and perceived risk of my ability to perform on the lease by simply prepaying the full term of the lease upfront or escrowing the full five years of rent at closing. That essentially eliminates the perceived risk on my ability to pay, thus making it a "guaranteed" income stream and a very safe investment for a potential buyer.

Eliminating tenant default risk by prepaying the full term of the master lease upfront justifies a major CAP rate compression, which increases market valuation of the property while NOI is held constant. In this case the value instantly went from a 10% CAP to a 7.25% CAP, resulting in a value increase from $1,500,000 to $2,750,000. With a $200,000 master lease prepaid upfront for five years ($1,000,000 in total), the net resulting cash proceeds were still only $1,750,000, which is slightly better than I could have gotten on the open market if I were to sell it as-is with existing tenants in place. But the difference is that now, I still get to keep the cash flow from my subtenants and keep 100% of the property cash flow for five more years. Additionally, I can possibly collect on the $1,000,000 or a portion of it, depending on how full I am able to keep the property over the next five years.

As-is Market Value of Building Before Master Lease	$1,500,000
As-is Market Cap Rate Without Master Lease	10.00%
Market CAP Rate with Fully Prepaid Master Lease	7.25%
Market Value with Prepaid Master Lease in Place	$2,750,000
Net Sale Proceeds after Prepaying Master Lease	$1,750,000
Extra Cash Gain at Closing	**$250,000**
Free Cashflow to be Collected for 5 years	**$200,000/year**

9

GROUND LEASES

"A building is a depreciating
liability; land is an appreciating asset."

BUILDINGS DO NOT APPRECIATE IN VALUE, ONLY LAND DOES

Regardless of where you live, you may have noticed the following trend in your city—a house near a major metropolitan
center that sold in 1975 for $25,000 is now worth $750,000 or
more. Yet a home of similar size, shape, and year in a different,
smaller city an hour away from a major metropolitan area
today is worth exactly the same or less than it was 30 years ago.
Such an observation inadvertently makes you wonder how
two nearly identical-sized, shaped, and year-of-construction
buildings in different cities or even in different neighborhoods
of the same city sell for drastically different prices.

The answer is rather simple—buildings do not change and do not increase in value over time; only the land does. As a matter of fact, the opposite is true—buildings in general actually depreciate in value over time and become obsolete. Materials that buildings are built out of (such as wood, flooring, paint, roofs, etc.) become worn out and tend to deteriorate over time. That is the reason why the Internal Revenue Service allows you to write off depreciation expenses on the buildings you own. In general, residential buildings can be depreciated to $0 value over 27.5 years, and commercial buildings can be depreciated to $0 value over 39 years. The Internal Revenue Service is also very specific. The only portion of your property that can be depreciated is the building and the improvements, not the land value.

Furthermore, the reason why certain similar-sized, shaped, and type-of-use properties are more desirable than others is due to the property's location, or rather the location of the land that the property sits on. That is the reason why waterfront properties in general are more expensive—it is because there is simply a limited supply of such desirable waterfront land. Understanding this real estate phenomenon can help you define your personal investment philosophy and guide you through your investment decisions about what properties to buy and keep, what properties to sell and why, or what properties to avoid altogether.

With that said, if your plan is to accumulate wealth over time through real estate ownership, it makes logical sense to focus your investment decisions on the appreciating portion of the assets you are considering buying, which by definition is land. However, land in general is hard to carry over time because it usually has no income stream. We have already discussed in earlier chapters possible ways to generate revenue from raw land. We will not discuss those ways again but rather focus on ways to accumulate urban infill land that have income-producing buildings on them to help carry the cost of land ownership over time.

Mobile home parks are a great way to "land bank" well-located, larger land parcels. Installing and renting mobile homes on your land is one of the oldest known ways to "land bank" land. However, most municipalities these days prohibit the construction of new mobile home parks unless you go a long ways outside of the city to a rural area, where appreciation and demand is not as high as in the inner-city of a metropolitan area. My personal preference, however, is to accumulate urban land that has the highest appreciation potential in my lifetime.

The best way to inexpensively acquire urban infill land with the highest potential for appreciation is to acquire it for the value of the current improvements that sit on it. Therefore, my goal would be to focus on inexpensive properties with inexpensive improvements that come with larger tracts of land. If you look at the overall spectrum of urban property types, you will quickly conclude that the least expensive ones are usually industrial ones.

Industrial properties are usually the least expensive type of commercial properties to build, yet they usually sit on the largest parcels of land, with large parking lots, large outdoor storage yards, and larger square footages of covered building areas. For example, in my city, $3,000,000 might buy you a small office or retail strip building 15,000 square feet in size that sits on one and a half acres of land. Yet the same $3,000,000 will also buy you a 50,000-square-foot industrial building that sits on five to seven acres of land.

Knowing that only land appreciates over time, my goal would be to own as much land as possible. So in the scenario above, if I had a limited supply of investment capital, my preference would be to buy the "inexpensive" industrial property that sits on a larger parcel of land every time over a more "expensive" and prestigious retail property. If properties that you are considering purchasing are located in close proximity to a major economic and employment center, then as the area grows and buildings become obsolete, they will inadvertently be slated for redevelopment. If the properties are sold in the future, they will likely be sold for the value of the land and not the buildings. Consequently, the larger the tract of land that sits underneath the buildings you are considering buying, the more valuable that property will eventually become.

Let's compare the two buildings from the scenario above and see what happens to their value over time. For purposes of this example, we will assume an average appreciation rate of five percent.

Retail Building

Total Purchase Price	$3,000,000
Land Size	1.5 acres
Building Size	15,000 sqft
Land Value	$475,000
Building Value	$2,525,000
Annual Appreciation Rate	5.00%
Value of Land in 20 years	$1,200,301
Value of Building in 20 years (if well maintained)	$2,525,000
Total Property Value in 20 years	**$3,725,000**

Industrial Building

Total Purchase Price	$3,000,000
Land Size	5.0 acres
Building Size	50,000 sqft
Land Value	$1,750,000
Building Value	$1,250,000
Annual Appreciation Rate	5.00%
Value of Land in 20 years	$4,422,163
Value of Building in 20 years (if well maintained)	$1,250,000
Total Property Value in 20 years	**$5,672,163**

Please note that these calculations assume buildings are exceptionally maintained to offset depreciation over time, and the original values of improvements are preserved at the same value without any depreciation. Other factors, such as rent growth, are generally tied to the location, and therefore any rent growth in the area is directly correlated to the land value, not the building value. Rising construction costs over time might affect the value of the improvements over time, but for purposes of this example, the construction cost on both retail and industrial properties would have similar pro rata increases in replacement costs that would not have an effect on the net differences in the value of improvements, especially if it's located near a high-growth metropolitan area.

NEVER SELL THE LAND, ONLY SELL THE BUILDINGS

I cannot say I ever regretted buying a piece of property, but I have for sure regretted selling properties. I especially regret selling super-infill, well-located buildings in Class A locations for one reason or another that seemed logical at the time. The problems that seemed big at the time that made me sell certain buildings, in hindsight, were truly insignificant. I wish I had figured out ways to hold on to those buildings. Having lived with a feeling of regret over selling certain assets has led me to make a declaration that I will never let that happen again—i.e., selling a well-located asset without the opportunity to forever own the land underneath the asset.

The reality of market economies, however, is such that occasionally we do have to sell assets for recapitalization, management purposes, financial, or non-financial reasons. The realization that only land appreciates over time and the feeling of regret of having sold certain buildings in the past have led me to come up with an ultimate investment strategy for myself, which I would also recommend for you. If you must sell something, only sell buildings. Never sell the land it sits on.

The strategy of separating buildings from the land and selling them independently of each other is a tool commonly known as ground leases. Ground leases are widely used among retailers and in the core urban centers but are less commonly seen in smaller markets. For example, over 500 acres of downtown Manhattan land sit on long-term ground leases. Most people assume that land and buildings go together, but the reality is that they do not have to go together. They can be divorced from one another through a deed of separation. In the world of investment real estate, where the value of assets is driven by CAP rates, in most cases you can actually increase the ultimate value of your asset by selling the building and land separately.

Here is an example of a mixed-use apartment building that I developed in my early 30s near North Carolina State University. It is a five-story, 16-unit student housing building with 49 beds and ground-floor retail.

The location of this asset is a A++. Having built it myself, I loved everything about this building. A Class A asset in a Class A location—it was a perfect candidate for a long-term hold. It is one of those properties that you die with and just place a deed restriction on that it cannot be sold outside of your trust for 100 years after your death. However, after a few years of ownership, I realized that because this building was built as a student housing project, it has proven to be rather management intensive to maintain and to keep long term.

I like the location aspect of it, but I do not like the work associated with managing 49 undergraduate students who live in it. So how can I keep the location but not have to deal with the rising property taxes, the insurance and utility costs, and the responsibilities of management and maintenance of the property? The answer is to sell the building on a ground lease. It cost a total of $5,400,000 to build, including $400,000 for the land; $400,000 on soft costs, architecture, and engineering; and $4,600,000 spent on construction and furnishings. Upon stabilization the building had an NOI of $420,000, putting its value at approximately $7,636,000, assuming a market CAP rate of 5.50% for the asset type at the time.

Property NOI	$420,000
Market CAP Rate	5.50%
Building Value	**$7,636,000**

The same improved asset type, but on a 99-year ground lease, would have a cap rate of roughly 50 basis points higher than a fee-simple asset, or approximately 6.0%. Conversely, ground-leased land under a high-quality improved asset like this would be considered an extremely low-risk investment and would trade at a sub-4% CAP rate, or approximately 150-200 basis points lower than a fee-simple combined price of the fee-simple property.

So if we were to separate the building from the land, we could sell it on a long-term ground lease to recoup our original investment of $5,400,000. To achieve such a price at a 6.00% CAP rate would require us to deliver a $324,000 NOI to a buyer, which leaves us $96,000 that we can charge for a ground lease rate.

Property NOI	$420,000
Less Ground Lease Payments	$96,000
Remaining NOI Net to Buyer	$324,000
Building NOI	$324,000
Market CAP Rate of Building	6.00%
Building Value	**$5,400,000**
Land NOI	$96,000
Market CAP Rate of Land	3.75%
Land Value	**$2,560,000**
Combined Property Value if Sold Separately	**$8,160,000**

An asset with the land and building sold separately will net on average 5-15% more than the same asset if sold fee simple from the beginning. If the asset is large enough, this strategy of separating the building and land may be worth the extra time and effort to sell them separately. That is, of course, if you really want to sell the asset in its entirety.

But more importantly, for the purposes of this chapter, this strategy enables you to recapitalize your investment and still keep the location and the land for long-term appreciation. It enables you to free yourself up from debt, from management, and from maintenance responsibilities of building upkeep but still maintain the cash flow in the form of ground lease payments. I believe I do not have to explain the benefits of owning free and clear properties with no management and no maintenance responsibilities that are producing passive cash flow every month. Having assets like these will result in an ultimate freedom for you and your family to do whatever you want in life and to travel wherever you want without having to physically attend to your properties every month.

A friend of mine from Canada has built an entire business around buying ground leases under office buildings. He has put together a large private equity fund whose entire investment strategy is to go to distressed (and non-distressed) building owners, get appraisals done on the land, and offer them a very attractive CAP rate to buy a 99-year ground lease underneath the building they own (5.00% CAP on average). The property owner gets to keep the building, but selling the land under it gives them an instant equity infusion to either pay off debt or perform capital improvements without a need to sell the whole asset.

His strategy is simple. Once he accumulates enough inventory of ground leases (maybe $5 billion worth), he plans to take it public in the form of a REIT and sell it at a very compressed CAP rate because of how low the perceived risk is in ground leases sitting under larger, expensive buildings. Based on other similar REITs currently trading on the public markets, he is projecting a 1 to 1.5% CAP rate on the exit.

If I had to do it all over again, I would never, ever sell any land I ever owned. I would only sell the buildings that sat on them. Looking back, land was never a problem. It was always something about the building maintenance or building management that I did not like.

Sometimes it is harder to find buyers to buy a property on a ground lease. That is why you have to discount the sale CAP rate by 50-100 basis points depending on the asset and location. But, more importantly, if you really think about it, you will realize that essentially all private properties in America are on unsubordinated ground leases with the government.

The term "fee simple" ownership is really deceiving, because you never truly own anything "fee simple."

If you do not pay your annual ground lease payment to your county's revenue department (i.e., if you do not pay your property taxes), you can be assured that they will be taking the property away from you. When I sell buildings on a long-term ground lease, I am essentially delivering the same property to the end user for a more affordable price, but with a higher property tax bill, or rather two property tax payments. One property tax is paid to a local municipality, like all properties do, and a second property tax is paid to me as the "fee simple" owner of the land it sits on.

10

DEPRECIATION & CONSERVATION

"Cost segregation analysis
is the best insurance
policy against missed 1031
exchanges."

DEPRECITIATION

One of the greatest benefits of owning commercial real estate is the tax shelter that it offers. The tax benefits that come with real estate ownership are the main reason this investment vehicle is so popular among the richest of the rich. The IRS allows you to amortize the value of residential and multifamily properties over 27.5 years and the value of commercial properties over 39 years. However, there is a way to significantly shorten this depreciation timeline to maximize the depreciation deduction (i.e., paper write-off) and to minimize tax on the front end to offset one's taxes. This can be accomplished by doing an engineering exercise commonly known as a cost segregation study.

Every building consists of many elements, such as paint, flooring, plumbing fixtures, elevators, roofs, siding, sidewalks, mechanical systems, etc. Not all of these components have the same useful life of 27.5 or 39 years. For example, a mechanical system (HVAC) might have a useful life of only 10 years, while paint on the walls may only have a useful life of five years before the building needs to be repainted again.

So a cost segregation study takes the building apart (figuratively speaking) based on its various components and applies different amortization schedules to the respective useful lives of its various components. In most cases it allows you to increase your depreciation deductions on the front end of building ownership to as much as 20-35% of the total building cost in your first year or two of ownership.

If you are purchasing buildings using leverage (most people do), and your down payment is 20-35% of the purchase price, the accelerated depreciation as described above can potentially equal or exceed the amount of your down payment. For example, if you have $1,000,000 of before-tax dollars and you do not buy a property with it, at the end of the year, you will have to pay taxes on it, somewhere around $350,000, depending on where you live. But if you use this $1,000,000 in pre-tax dollars to put a 25% down payment on a $4,000,000 property, and you then perform a cost segregation analysis for accelerated depreciation, you can potentially generate enough first-year write-offs to offset your entire $1,000,000 gain and wipe out your entire tax obligation through doing this exercise.

Taxable Income Before Investment Purchase	$1,000,000
Tax Obligation (35% Tax Rate)	$350,000
Downpayment to buy $4,000,000 building	$1,000,000
Paper Loss Created thru Cost Segregation Study	-$1,000,000
Net Resulting Taxable Income	$0.00
Ending Tax Obligation (35% Tax Rate)	**$0.00**

It is important to note that when you go to sell the property, you will ultimately have to pay back the depreciation recapture tax, but the same holds true if you were to follow a normal depreciation schedule and accelerated depreciation timeline.

With all of this said, I would also like to emphasize that I am not a licensed accountant, licensed attorney, or tax professional, and the information provided herein is anecdotal in nature and shall not be construed as me providing legal, accounting, or tax advice. You should always seek a professional's advice to assess the legal and tax ramifications of your particular situation.

CONSERVATION EASEMENTS

Conservation easements are another great tool that should be present in the arsenal of tools of every real estate investor. A conservation easement is a voluntary legal agreement where a landowner restricts future development on their property by "selling" or donating the development rights to a land trust or government agency, essentially protecting the land's natural or agricultural values in perpetuity.

Conservation easements are most commonly used on raw land where the property owner uses the land for personal recreational purposes, such as hunting or farmland, and does not plan to redevelop it. By placing a conservation easement on the land, the property owner still gets to use the property for his or her intended use (recreation) but can get a large tax deduction of up to 90% or more of the land's value to offset taxes.

If you are purchasing a 20-acre piece of land for recreational use and it costs you $1,000,000 based on the prices of land in your area, by placing a conservation easement on the land, you might be able to get as much as 90% of your purchase price back as paper losses to offset your future gains.

While conservation easements are most frequently utilized on rural land, there are uncommon ways where conservation easements can be used effectively in an urban setting with fully developed buildings. A good example of the application of this tool would be one of my office buildings in downtown Raleigh.

The subject property is a five-story building located in the central business district of the city. The zoning in this area allows for buildings up to 40 stories in height. Due to the size of the parcel (0.06 acres), I do not believe it will be practical to demolish the existing five-story building to rebuild a 40-story building in its place, so I do not think this property will ever be redeveloped into its maximum density potential of a 40-story tower. Therefore, this property presents a perfect opportunity to place a conservation easement on it to prevent the development of an extra 35 stories on top of the existing five.

In this particular case, DX-40 zoned land as of the date of this publication is selling around $460/sqft, or around $20,000,000 per acre. So the land portion of the total value of this property is approximately $1,200,000. By placing a conservation easement limiting future development rights not to exceed five stories in height, it can be argued that we restricted 87.5% of the land's future use, which resulted in a loss of value in the amount of $1,050,000. The best part is that when you go to sell this property in the future, this conservation easement on height will not have any effect on the resale price of the property. So this $1,050,000 of paper losses is pure found money created literally from "thin air."

While cost segregation studies and conservation easements do not directly affect your NOI or CAP rate, they are great tools to use to keep more dollars in your pocket at the end of the day by creating carry-forward paper losses to offset your gains. Remember that there are two sides to making money—earning it and keeping it. Keeping it is usually more important.

Conclusion

"Knowledge without
application is nothing more
than entertainment."

Real estate has unlimited expandability potential to improve cash flow, create equity, and build significant wealth. More often than not, these potentials are present in plain sight. However, to recognize potential areas of expandability and to capitalize on such opportunities, it requires seeing beyond what is visible to the naked eye. That is why if you choose real estate investing as a means of wealth creation, and especially if you decide upon real estate as your career path, you need to become educated not on just one aspect of real estate, but on as many as you possibly can.

Most people know of just one way to make money in real estate—buy low, sell high. But in highly competitive markets, it is virtually impossible to find real estate that can be bought with deep discounts. To make money in such markets requires knowledge of many real estate tools that can be utilized to compete in such highly competitive markets. Some investors may also know, or at least have heard of, some other real estate tools such as right of first refusal, options, lease options, subject-to's, seller financing, sale-leasebacks, substitution of security, subordination agreements, partial note releases, releases without satisfaction, all-inclusive trust deeds, wrap notes, debt buy-downs, equity swaps and splits, private placement memorandums, crowdfunding, etc.

All of these are "real estate tools" that can be used to recognize opportunity, be competitive, and make money in highly competitive markets. But please note that even this entire variety is still just a few tools that I use for example purposes. The real estate industry has thousands of tools!

The more tools you know and become educated and proficient with, the more opportunities you will be able to recognize, and the more creatively you will be able to structure your deals. That is why if you choose real estate as your wealth creation vehicle, you better become educated not on just one or two tools but on *all* of the options that are available in the real estate industry.

The sport of real estate acquisition is a huge money sport. We deal with hundreds of thousands or millions of dollars with everything we do in the real estate world. Education is tough. Studying thousands of real estate topics and strategies is tiring and time-consuming. But think about it in terms of what it means to you financially. Once you answer that question for yourself, it can make your education process much more pleasant. If one tool you learn can help you improve your real estate investing performance by 1%, then it's probably time and money well spent.

If I buy a small apartment building for $3.4 million, and I have thought of everything there is to think about because I have taken the time to educate myself. I have accounted for all factors. I have thought about and factored in everything there is to know. I am 99% there, but I make a 1% mistake—what does it cost me? Is it not $34,000?

What if I'm developing a $12,000,000 shopping center and I make a 1% or 2% mistake on my development cost estimates? You get the point. Consider the price of ignorance. It is much more expensive than the price of education. I commend you on taking time to read this book, because you obviously recognize the value of continuing education. Sounds funny, coming from a guy with no formal education.

The most successful real estate entrepreneurs I know never stop learning, reading, or studying new topics, trends, and strategies of real estate investing. The most successful real estate entrepreneurs I know with eight- or nine- figure net worths have forgotten more than most people know about real estate investing, yet I can find them attending a real estate seminar in some part of the country any given month of the year. Why do those people spend time away from their business and their family when they have already amassed incredible wealth and have forgotten more than 99% of the people will ever know about real estate investing? The answer is rather simple—recognizing opportunities does not require luck. It requires education and preparedness. Successful people define luck as preparedness meeting opportunity. One will not be able to utilize their "luck" when an opportunity presents itself if they are not prepared and do not possess the appropriate knowledge to take advantage of the opportunity.

The truth of the matter is that there are actually four types of luck—blind luck, hustle luck, smart luck, and quantum luck. While the first one, blind luck, is leaving things to a random game of chance and is outside of our control, the other three types of luck are more common in everyday life and are 100% within our own control to create. Hustle luck simply means the harder I work, the luckier I get. I am sure you have heard this before. Smart luck is a step above it and means working smarter instead of harder. Smart luck comes into play when you hustle long enough that you start doing pattern recognitions that are more likely to result in you getting "lucky." Lastly, quantum luck is when you get so good at what you do that luck finds you by itself, and you just attract it from the universe.

Unsuccessful people generally categorize all the successes of others under blind luck as an excuse for their own failure. What they are blind to see, however, is that successful people often have more failures than less successful people do. They just keep going, and they never quit.

The misperception around the term luck arises when people hear about so-called incredible overnight successes that are happening every day in our society, and they start to believe that overnight success is indeed possible, with blind luck playing a part. While luck may have been involved, it was certainly not the blind one. That is the instant-gratification syndrome that we have talked about earlier. I cannot tell you how many times I have heard people tell me, "Oh, Nikita, of course it's easy for you, because you are just so lucky."

What they really hear is a bottom-line result, such as I made $1,000,000 on a quick flip after one day of ownership. What they do not hear are the months or possibly years of entitlement work, diligent effort, and sweat equity that I or another company or an individual like me might have put up front into the property while they had it under option agreement, investing money into engineering, architectural, soil borings, environmental consultants, and rezoning attorneys along the way. They also do not hear about the years or decades of sweat equity that a person or a company has spent, without being paid a penny along the way, while educating themselves on different subjects and the tools necessary for the successful execution of a venture-producing, multimillion-dollar profit in one swoop on the back end.

This leads people to unrealistic expectations and results in disappointment when they fail to realize their goals. Based on my experience and observations, I have concluded that an average "overnight success" takes 10 years to achieve.

In conclusion, I would like to say that life is too important to rely on blind luck. You and only you are responsible for your destiny, and you can create the reality of your dreams if you just learn how to create things from the quantum field instead of from physical matter. You cannot simply react to obstacles that arise on your road to success. You need to educate yourself on various tools available to you as a real estate entrepreneur to be able to walk around the barriers you encounter along the way and turn them into profit. And when you get knocked down (and you absolutely will sooner or later), you need to get back up. Every successful CEO you will ever read about has been knocked down at one point in his or her life. The key is to not get discouraged, get back up, and keep going. It's hard to beat someone that never quits.

Remember that successful people create their own luck by endlessly educating themselves on tools that are important to their business and so should you. I, myself, am a great believer in "luck." The harder, smarter, and deeper in the quantum I work, the luckier I get!

Good luck in all your endeavors!!!

SUGGESTIONS FOR MAXIMIZING YOUR CASH FLOW AND EQUITIES

In every property you own or are considering purchasing, always look for the following factors that most people do not pay attention to:

1. Who is paying utilities—the landlord or tenant? Can the utilities be submetered or can the utility costs be passed down to tenants in your building to optimize NOI?

2. What is the tax assessed value of your property and could there be reasons to justify a tax appeal?

3. Does the building have any special significance in terms of its historical, prehistorical, architectural, archaeological, and/or cultural importance that can possibly justify a landmark designation for a tax reduction?

4. Does it have parking that can be rented for additional revenue?

5. Is there any extra space such as a basement or a retail or pedestrian frontage that can be utilized for ATM machines, coin operated laundry, or vending?

6. Is roof space being utilized efficiently for NOI optimization with measures such as cell-tower leases or solar panels?

7. Is there extra land on the property that can be utilized for a billboard or traditional cell-tower lease?

8. If you own or are considering purchasing raw land, does it have mature timber that can be harvested? Does your property have the potential to mine or lease out for mineral, farming, or hunting rights?

9. What is the current zoning for the property and future land use plan for the area? Is there an opportunity for rezoning or entitling the land for its higher and better use?

10. Have you studied rent comps in your area for your asset type and is your subject building getting fair market rents?

A PIECE OF WISDOM FROM THE AUTHOR

The sport of real estate acquisition has allowed me and many people like me to achieve extraordinary financial success and freedom. I am confident that you, too, can realize greater success in your life and business through the use of the powerful tools described in this book, tools that may be hiding in your plain sight. The toolbox of real estate is practically endless, and these are just a few of my favorite strategies as they require a minimal out-of-pocket cash outlay. If used correctly, these tools will help you multiply your net worth at lightning speed.

Remember that real estate is a team sport, and without a strong and loyal team around you, you will not be able to achieve one-tenth of the success that you otherwise could. Build a strong team to complement your business, such as your attorneys, engineers, and other professional advisors.

Also, real estate is a people business, and therefore your focus in this business should be first and foremost on the people and not just on the properties. Properties do not make decisions for themselves to sell themselves to you at favorable terms. The people who own them do. So focus on people. We become an average of the top five to 10 people that we spend the most time with over the course of a six to 12 month period. So choose carefully who you surround yourself with, because they will ultimately shape who you become.

In your personal life, likewise, invest in those who invest in you and stay loyal to you. People in your business and in your personal life will ultimately shape and define who you are, and if you have the right people around you, they will help you realize everything you have ever dreamed of in your life.

AUTHOR'S GUIDING PRINCIPLES OF LIFE AND BUSINESS

Everything that I have learned from all my mentors, from all the books I have read, from the school of hard knocks, and from my roller coaster rides in real estate business can be boiled down to the following simple philosophies, which now have become my guiding principles in life and in business.

42 Guiding Principles in Real Estate:

1. Never sell land; only sell buildings.

2. Find the best way to make money and do not deviate from it.

3. Less is more. Having fewer buildings with low debt is better than having many buildings with higher debt.

4. Cash flow is key to sustainability in times of recession.

5. Keep overhead low. Having a lean operation gives you a longer runway to sustain a recession.

6. Create multiple sources of income, one for every reoccurring expense in life.

7. The answer to every question you do not ask is an automatic and definite no. Simply make the offer that

works for you.

8. Always be marketing. You need pawns in your real estate portfolio in order to protect your back row pieces for long-term hold.

9. It's a people business, so always try to get face-to-face with people.

10. Make a lot of offers. Making offers is like playing a free lottery.

11. Money is never the reason why people sell properties. Search for non-cash solutions to problems.

12. Structures never appreciate, only land does. Accumulate large tracks of land with inferior structures in good locations.

13. Always ask this question—is it a people problem or a property problem?

14. Vacancy is cancer. Get rid of it before it kills you.

15. Negative cash flow is a finite number. Get rid of negative cash flow as soon as possible.

16. Time kills all deals; strike while the iron is hot.

17. Send a thank you note after every meeting. Kindness and gratitude go a long ways.

18. In a long-term hold property, the price you pay is the

least important component of a transaction.

19. Instead of competing, partner with competitors and turn them into your allies.

20. Offer value to people for free; they tend to reciprocate more.

21. Know everyone in your world. The answer is usually right in front of you.

22. Take care of properties and eventually they will take care of you.

23. The best deals are "engineered," not "found."

24. Mentors are available for the price of asking.

25. ABD—Always be Disclosing

26. If you are going to think anyway, you might as well think big.

27. When making investment decisions, it's either a "wow, hell yes," or it's a no.

28. Saying yes to "kind of cool" projects is the most sure way to go out of business quickly.

29. Learn to say no in one word.

30. The direction you are heading is more important than how fast you are going.

31. All real benefits in life come from compound interest. Leverage the compound nature of NOI and CAP rates to multiply your wealth in real estate.

32. Most businesses die not from starvation but from indigestion. Do not bite off more than you can chew (aka do not take on too many projects at once).

33. If you don't see yourself working with someone for the rest of your life, don't work with them for a day.

34. No business rewards more for education and penalizes more for lack thereof than real estate. Never stop learning. Ignorance is much more expensive than the price of education.

35. In the age of information technology such as Google, ignorance is a choice.

36. There are two sides to making money—earning it and keeping it. Keeping it is more important. The best way to start making money is to stop losing money. The best way to improve your life is to stop messing it up.

37. The opportunity of a lifetime must be seized during the lifetime of the opportunity. Timing is everything.

38. Action cures fear. Overcome fears with math and market knowledge.

39. Under promise and over deliver.

40. Dance with people, not with properties.

41. The greatest plan will not work if you will not.

42. Create deals; don't compete for them.

55 Guiding Principles of Life:

1. You are responsible for your own life. Extreme ownership and 100% responsibility for your life is the only
   way to end suffering and persevere in life.

2. The key to happiness is to learn to enjoy the present
   moment. Don't think about the past or the future. All
   possibilities exist in the generous present moment, the
   eternal now. Don't get caught up in ideas and miss the
   miracle called life.

3. Life is fair by being unfair to everyone. Don't fall into
   victimhood. No one cares anyway, so take charge of
   your own destiny to create a life you want for yourself.

4. The mind may think, but the heart knows. The door
   to your future lives in your heart. Always follow your
   heart. Closing your heart because you have been hurt
   in the past only blocks your own flow of energy.

5. Hurt people hurt people. If you are angry with yourself, you'll be angry with others. If you are happy with
   yourself, you'll be happy with others. When you are
   unhappy in life, start by looking in the mirror.

6. There is no way to happiness; happiness is the way.

7. Do not wait for wealth to feel abundance. Do not wait
   for love to feel loved and happy. You cannot wait for

life to change to feel the emotion. You have to feel the emotion first for your life to change.

8. The key to survival is in your ability to adopt to change quickly. What got you here won't get you there. Keep evolving.

9. There are no mistakes, just lessons. Use pain to find clarity. Pain is the best teacher.

10. Doing is more important than doing well. You can't steer a parked car. If you have a business idea, just get in motion and start doing it. You will figure out the right path along the way.

11. By giving love freely, we become spiritual millionaires. It is not enough to just be a financial millionaire; you have to be spiritual one too.

12. Protect your body as a temple. It is the only home we do not choose. Treat your food as medicine. Otherwise you will eat your medicine as food. If you do not make time for exercise, you will eventually make time for illness.

13. The more value you create for the community, the more the community will pay you for this value. You should always strive to become the best version of yourself and be resourceful when resources are needed.

14. Meditation is the most important practice you can do

for your health. All the unhappiness of men comes from their inability to sit in silence with themselves.

15. We all get what we tolerate. If you want extraordinary life, stop tolerating mediocrity.

16. Your network equals your net worth.

17. Wanting is better than having. Enjoy the process.

18. Change is never a matter of ability; change is a matter of motivation.

19. If you are not happy in a relationship, it means you have too many rules.

20. Do not vouch for people or things that are outside of your control.

21. Do not judge others if you do not want to be judged yourself. There is always another side of the story. Just ask to tell the story.

22. All significant change has a precursor of disgust. Frustration means you are about to have a major breakthrough.

23. Your personality creates your personal reality. If want to create a new reality for yourself, change your personality, change your energy, change the scenery, change your routine, change the road you drive to work, change your habits, etc. Nothing changes until you change. If you do not change anything, your past

will be your future.

24. A man who does not read is no different than a man who cannot read. Your mind is a muscle that needs constant exercise. The difference between the people you admire and everyone else is that the former read. Pattern recognition requires constantly feeding the brain with updated information. People who read live 1000 lives, people who do not live only one.

25. Imagination is more important than knowledge. Put no limits on imagination. Worry is a misuse of imagination.

26. By being hard on yourself, it makes it harder for others to be hard on you. When you are tough on yourself, life will be infinitely easier on you.

27. An ounce of prevention is worth a pound of cure. Kill problems at inception, while they are still small.

28. Suffering ceases to be suffering when it finds meaning. When going through tough times, try to identify a lesson you are supposed to learn from that experience, and as soon as you are able to pinpoint it, it ceases to cause you pain.

29. An extraordinary life only exists outside your comfort zone. We do not grow inside our comfort zone, we do not learn in our comfort zone, we do not get stretched in our comfort zone, and we certainly do not make mistakes in our comfort zone. Mistakes often become

our greatest assets!

30. All problems can be avoided by asking more and better questions.

31. The only way to make your present better is to make your future bigger. Keep remembering your future. Tell people the story of your future, not your past.

32. No one can make you feel inferior without your permission. Your value does not change based on someone's inability to see your worth.

33. Tough situations do not build your character, they reveal it.

34. If not on the day I die, then not today either.

35. Be yourself, everyone else is taken.

36. Few things in life stay important over a continuous period of time. Don't waste time on worry.

37. The game is lost or won between two ears.

38. Whether you say you can or you can't, you are absolutely right.

39. The only thing that stands between you and your goals is a meaningful conversation.

40. We over estimate what we can do in one year and under estimate what we can in five years.

41. Learn to love what others would not tolerate. Do what others would not for five years, and you can do what others cannot for the rest of your life.

42. Success is a journey, not a destination. Enjoy the sweat, the blood, and the tears of the process.

43. Keep life simple. Learn how to communicate with people in fifth-grade language.

44. Live within your means, and put the rest to work.

45. Success is not what you have, but what you do with what you have.

46. The secret to life is being kind. Always be nice to people; someday you will need them.

47. Everyone is fighting a battle that no one knows about. Be compassionate and kind to everyone.

48. Fear is temporary; regret is forever.

49. Today is the tomorrow you visualized or feared yesterday.

50. It's important to remember a low point in your life to avoid repeating the mistakes that led you there. Scar tissue is a very valuable asset; never forget it.

51. Always stay calm.

52. Fail, fail, fail will eventually turn into win, win, win. Fail

faster.

53. Outwork your competition—grind harder, hustle smarter.

54. The definition of hell is meeting a person you could have been. Make sure you do not meet that person in your lifetime.

55. Do not take anything you have in life for granted. You are exactly three "missiles" away from being a homeless man on the corner of a street with a sign.

ABOUT THE AUTHOR

Nikita S. Zhitov was born in Novosibirsk, Russia, in 1985. He immigrated to the United States with his family in 2000 at the age of 14. Nikita graduated from the North Carolina School of Science and Mathematics at the age of 18 in 2004, where he began his career in real estate investing. After attending the University of North Carolina at Chapel Hill on a full scholarship for a short period of time, Nikita dropped out of the university to pursue a career in real estate investing full time.

Since the beginning of his investment career, Nikita has brokered, acquired, master-leased, and developed hundreds of properties in the continental United States. His experience in the industry includes historic apartment building renovations, ground-up construction of mixed-use and multifamily projects, land development, ground-up development of single- and multi-tenant retail buildings, the acquisition and renovation of office buildings, build-to-suit and ground lease transactions with national and publicly traded retail tenants, residential subdivision developments, condo conversions, mineral rights exploitation, mobile home parks, and luxury housing construction.

Today Nikita lives with his family in North Carolina. He is recognized as a local business leader, an industry expert, and an expert motivational speaker. He continues to own and operate his real estate investment company, Cityplat LLC, specializing in the acquisition of value-add small bay industrial and neighborhood retail centers throughout the Southeast.

www.ingramcontent.com/pod-product-compliance
Lightning Source LLC
Chambersburg PA
CBHW040857210326
41597CB00029B/4874